# The Mother of Imām al-Mahdī

## An Exposition Into Her Identity



Shaykh Aḥmad Salmān

AL-BURĀQ

# Copyright



ISBN: 978-1-956276-49-7
Printed and published by al-Burāq Publications.
Translated and annotated by al-Burāq Publications. Where needed, context and transliterations were added. Some minor edits were made to the translated Arabic text.



www.al-Buraq.org
publications@al-Buraq.org

First Edition | May 2024

# Dedication

The publication of this book was made possible through the generous support of our donors.

Please recite *Sūrat al-Fātihah* and ask God for the Divine reward (*thawāb*) to be conferred upon the donors and also the souls of all the deceased in whose memory their loved ones have contributed graciously towards the publication of *The Mother of Imām al-Mahdī: An Exposition Into Her Identity.*

We begin by giving all praise and thanks to God ﷻ for giving us the *tawfiq* to translate this book. He has guided us and without Him, we would not have been guided to the straight path embodied by the Prophet Muḥammad ﷺ and the Ahl al-Bayt عليهم السلام.

This book is dedicated to all the scholars, martyrs and believers who worked tirelessly to promote the pure Muḥammadan path.

We want to also give our thanks and appreciation to all believers from around the world and acknowledge the team which helped al-Burāq Publications complete this work, spending countless hours to make its publication possible. Please recite Sūrat al-Fātiḥah on behalf of them, their families, and their marḥūmīn.

This book is dedicated in honor of the following individuals. Please remember them in your prayers and may God ﷻ have mercy on them and their loved ones.

Abbas Yassine

Abdul Ali Shaltouki

Abu Banat Mujahid

Ali Adam Mehdi

Ali Ftouni

Ali Hammoud

Ali Khoyee

Alvina Nichols

Alya Agemy

Amatul Fatima Razvi

Amina Begum

Ansia Naqvi

Asa Alassad

Āyatullāh Sayyid Muḥammad Riḍā Shīrāzī

Ayesha Saddique

Bande Khuda

Bilqees Zehra

Ghada Mohanna

Ghadir Amanda Gharib

Hajj Abou Kassem El Cheikh Ali

Hajj Adel Kobeissi

Hajj Hassan Sobh

Hajj Sami Ftouni

Hajji Amneh Sobh-Ftouni

Hajji Hiam Hojeije

Mirza Mazher A. Baig

Mirza Yaseen H. Kizilbash

Mohamed Hussain Mussa

Munawwar Jehan

Musharaf Husain

Najeebe Ammar

Naz Fatima

Nouran Alyousif

Omeed Rezaian

Rayhan Alyousif

Rayhana Hammoud

Razia Sarfaraz

Rukhaiya Begum

Saghir Fatima

Sami Saleh

Sarah Ikrabat

Sayyid Khaled Abdallah

Sayyid Sobh H. Sobh

Semin Balkhi

Shandaar Fatima

Soad Naeem

Somayyeh Farazandeh

Syed Ajaz Moosavi

Syed Asad Jafri

Syed Fidvi Ali

Hajji Iman Elsaghir
Hajji Imane Srour
Hajji Intissar Bazzi
Halema Ibrahim
Hasan Jahan Qamar
Hassan Yassine
Hosain H. Rizvi
Hussain Raza
Juman Alyousif
Kaneez Batool Kizilbash
Karar Albayati
Khadija Fawaz
Khadija Shoaib
Khanum Rabab
Mahmoud Tiba
Mallak Jaber
Manonda Lattimore
Masooma Begum
Massih Seyedmadani
Mirza Ahmed A. Baig
Syed Jaffar Nawaz Hussain
Syed Mehdi Ahmed
Syed Mehdi H. Rizvi
Syed Mujtaba Ahmed
Syed Mumtaz A. Gilani
Syed Nadeem A. Gilani
Syed Nawab R. Kazmi
Syeda Asghari
Syeda Baqueri
Syeda Batool
Syeda Jafri
Syeda Masooma Begum
Tahereh Esfahani
Taqia Naqvi
Turfah Sobh
Yasmin Banatwala
Yousuf Ali Rizvi
Zahraa Hammoud
Zainul Abedin Abbas
Zakieh Charaf Aldine

# Du'ā' al-Ḥujjah

اللّهُمَّ كُنْ لِوَلِيِّكَ الحُجَّةِ بْنِ الحَسَنِ صَلَواتُكَ

عَلَيْهِ وَعَلى آبائِهِ في هذِهِ السّاعَةِ وَفي كُلِّ

ساعَةٍ وَلِيّاً وَحافِظاً وَقائِداً وَناصِراً وَدَليلاً

وَعَيْناً حَتّى تُسْكِنَهُ أَرْضَكَ طَوْعاً وَتُمَتِّعَهُ فيها طَويلاً

O God, be, for Your representative, the Ḥujjat (proof), son of al-Ḥasan, Your blessings be upon him and his forefathers, in this hour and in every hour: a guardian, a protector, a leader, a helper, a proof, and an eye - until You make him live on the Earth, in obedience (to You), and cause him to live in it for a long time.

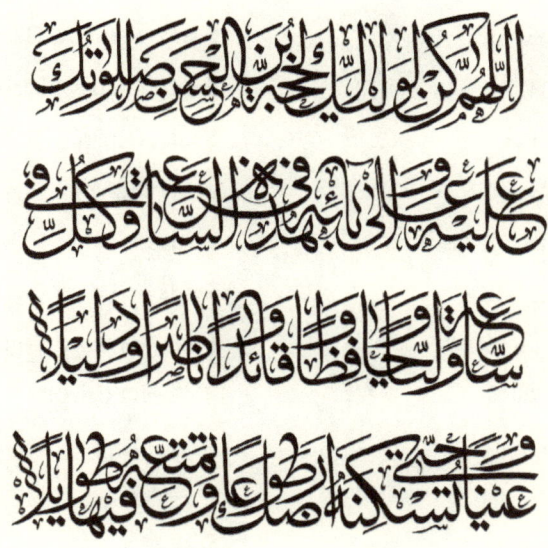

# Terms of Respect

The following Arabic phrases have been used throughout this book in their respective places to show the reverence which the noble personalities deserve.

عزّ وجلّ

Used for God, meaning:
*Exalted and Sublime (Perfect) is He*

صلى الله عليه وآله

Used for Prophet Muḥammad, meaning:
*Blessings from God be upon him and his family*

عليه السلام

Used for a man (singular) of a high status, meaning:
*Peace be upon him*

عليها السلام

Used for a woman (singular) of a high status, meaning:
*Peace be upon her*

عليهما السلام

Used for men/women (dual) of a high status, meaning:
*Peace be upon them both*

عليهم السلام

Used for men and/or women (plural) of a high status, meaning:
*Peace be upon them all*

عجّل الله تعالى فرجه الشريف

Used for Imām Muḥammad al-Mahdī, meaning:
*May God hasten his return*

قدّس سرّه

Used for a deceased scholar, meaning:
*May his resting [burial] place remain pure*

# Transliteration Table

The method of transliteration of Islamic terminology from the Arabic language has been carried out according to the standard transliteration table below.

| | | | | | |
|---|---|---|---|---|---|
| ء | ʾ | ر | r | ف | f |
| ا | a | ز | z | ق | q |
| ب | b | س | s | ك | k |
| ت | t | ش | sh | ل | l |
| ث | th | ص | ṣ | م | m |
| ج | j | ض | ḍ | ن | n |
| ح | ḥ | ط | ṭ | و | w |
| خ | kh | ظ | ẓ | ه | h |
| د | d | ع | ʿ | ي | y |
| ذ | dh | غ | gh | | |
| **Long Vowels** | | | | | |
| ا | ā | و | ū | ي | ī |
| **Short Vowels** | | | | | |
| ــَـ | a | ــُـ | u | ــِـ | i |

# Table of Contents

# Introduction

بسم الله الرحمن الرحيم

*In the Name of God, the Beneficent, the Merciful*

Praise be to God, the Beneficent, the Merciful, and peace and blessings be upon the noblest of prophets and messengers, Muḥammad ﷺ and his pure, infallible progeny عليهم السلام.

Undoubtedly, research on the mothers of the infallible Imāms عليهم السلام is necessary and closely linked to the Ahl al-Bayt's biography عليهم السلام. Not only did their enemies seek to smear and distort the biography of the Holy Imāms عليهم السلام, but they also worked to do the same to their mothers, whose biographies have been subject to many distortions, alterations, and manipulations.

Perhaps the biography of Lady Narjis عليها السلام, the mother of Imām Muḥammad al-Mahdī, is surrounded by significant ambiguity and confusion, as contradictions and differences are ingrained in all the matters related to her such that even the truth of her name is muddled. This led some transgressors to link her with different figures, and some even crossed the lines of decency and attributed to her that which a believer must not mention due to some things narrated about her life.

Therefore, this small book is my attempt to gather all that is narrated about this virtuous lady عليها السلام from the books of ḥadīth, history, and biographies and thus eliminate the ambiguity that has surrounded her so that the reader can acquire an image of her ﷺ life and, more importantly, her role in the al-Mahdī movement, particularly in the minor occultation of the Imām of the Time ﷺ.

Shaykh Aḥmad Salmān

1 Jumādā al-Ūlā 1442 AH

# Her Naming

Among the books of history, biographies, and biographers, we find a significant dispute in naming the mother of our master and guardian, the Imām of the Time عجل الله فرجه الشريف. In this regard, all of the following names were given to her among the various accounts:

- Narjis
- Sawsan
- Rayḥāna
- Ṣāqīl
- Malīka
- Khamt
- Ḥakīmah
- Maryam

Some even employed this dispute to discredit the cause of al-Mahdī عجل الله فرجه الشريف; one such transgressor mentioned this dispute among what he called "contradictions in the life of the Shīʿa's awaited Mahdī", where he said,

> "Who is the Mahdī's mother? Is she a slave girl called Narjis, Ṣāqīl, Malīka, Khamt, Ḥakīmah, Rayḥāna, or Sawsan, or is she a free woman named Maryam?"[1]

Similarly, another commented on this dispute:

> "How is his existence known and certain when there is such uncertainty regarding his mother?... Notice this answer's weakness and immense affectation, seeking to dodge much of the contradictions surrounding this figure [the Mahdī]."[2]

Therefore, it is prudent that we clarify the truth of the matter.

## Are These Names Firmly Established?

First, it is essential to discuss whether these names are deeply rooted [in our literature] and historically accurate, as some names do not have any valid origin at all!

For example, it is only Ibn Khallikān who claimed that one of her names is "Khamt", saying

> "He was born on a Friday night in the middle of Shaʿbān in the year 255 AH, and his father died when

[1] al-Kharāshī, Sulaymān b. Ṣāliḥ, *As'ilat Qadat al-Shabāb al-Shīʿa ilā al-Ḥaqq*, p. 68.

[2] *Matā Yushriq Nūruka Ayyuhā al-Muntaẓar*, p. 34.

> he was five years old. His mother's name is Khamt, and it is also said that her name is Narjis. The Shīʿa say that he entered the basement in his father's home while his mother looked on, and he never returned to her. This happened in 265 AH when he was nine years old."[3]

This man does not believe in what he narrates about the holy progeny and the history of the Shīʿa; undoubtedly, the man's fraudulent writings and animosity towards Ahl al-Bayt ﷺ were long proven, and this is evident in the following two points:

First: The reason why he was known as Ibn Khallikān is that he was excessively proud of his ancestors, and so he would always say, "My father was so and so," "My grandfather was so and so," "My ancestors were so and so," and so on. People used to say to him: "Leave [what is in] the past alone[4] and talk about yourself [instead]." This eventually became his nickname.

Similarly, Ibn al-ʿImād al-Ḥanbalī narrated the following on the authority of one of his shaykhs:

> "Among his testimonies is that the name Ibn Khallikān was coined from two Arabic verbs: *Khalli* something

---

[3] Ibn Khallikān, *Wafayāt al-Aʿyān wa-Anbāʾ Abnāʾ al-Zamān*, Vol. 4, p. 176.

[4] Khalli kāna transliterated in Arabic; notice how his name (Khallikān) is a juxtaposition of this phrase.

[to give up on a matter or leave it aside] and *Kāna* [verb that indicates the past]. That is because he would always say, 'my father was [*Kāna*] so and so', 'my grandfather was so and so', and so on; thus, he was told to leave such matters behind [*Khalli Kāna*], and he eventually became known for it [and thus the name]."[5]

Referring to this man's history, we find that he is of Barmakid ancestry, and whoever is familiar with history knows certainly that the Barmakids harbored the most animosity towards the ʿAlawīyūn [herein and onwards, the word ʿAlawī refers to the Shīʿa at that time, the followers of Imām ʿAlī b. Abī Ṭālib 🌼, the Ahl al-Bayt 🌸 and the holy progeny, and not to the deviant sect of Nuṣayrīs]. The Barmakids were the iron fist of the ʿAbbāsid dynasty in its early days. The ʿAbbāsids relied on them because they [the ʿAbbāsids] did not trust the Arabs and Ajam due to their sympathy for the ʿAlawīyūn. This sympathy for the ʿAlawīyūn stems from the ʿAbbāsids' betrayal of the pledge to give the Caliphate to Imām ʿAlī al-Riḍā 🌼 from the progeny of the Holy Prophet 🌼 if they succeeded in overthrowing the Umayyad dynasty. Instead, they monopolized the rule. Thus, the Barmakids became the steel sword that persecuted the enemies of the ʿAbbāsids, particularly the ʿAlawīyūn.

---

[5] al-Ḥanbalī, Ibn al-ʿImād, *Shadharāt al-Dhahab fī Akhbār Man Dhahab*, Vol. 8, p. 422.

As such, we conclude that a history of animosity is deep-rooted between the Barmakids and the ʿAlawīyūn, and we thus do not doubt that the words of Ibn Khallikān stem from this hatred.

Furthermore, Ibn Khallikān adored Yazīd b. Muʿāwīya b. Abī Sufyān and his poetry fiercely. In the translation of *al-Marzubānī*, the following is mentioned:

> "...[Ibn Khallikān] was the first to compile the collection of Yazīd b. Muʿāwīya b. Abī Sufyān al-Umayyad and take care of it. It was a small collection, the size of about three booklets. Afterward, some people added many things that did not belong to him. I [Ibn Khallikān] had memorized the entire collection of Yazīd—due to my adoration for him—in the year 633 in Dimashq [Damascus], and I had thus come to know what was rightly attributed to him and what was not. I continued investigating until I identified the author of every verse, and I would have shown this in detail were it not for the sake of brevity. Nonetheless, Yazīd's poetry is excellent even though it is only a few poems."[6]

What is the reason behind Ibn Khallikān's fierce admiration of Yazīd's poetry?

On the one hand, if his love was for the content of the poetry, then this is an indicator of the foul nature of Ibn

---

[6] Ibn Khallikān, *Wafayāt al-Aʿyān wa-Anbāʾ Abnāʾ al-Zamān*, Vol. 4, p. 354.

Khallikān as Yazīd's works were not poems dedicated to the remembrance of God ﷻ or the praise of His Prophet ﷺ. Instead, his poetry was the epitome of corruption and immorality. In this regard, al-Dhahabī best summarized the life of Yazīd b. Mu'āwīya b. Abī Sufyān when he said,

> "He [Yazīd] was a Nāṣibī, rude, repulsive, ill-mannered, drunkard, and wrong-doer, and he established his government upon killing the martyr [Imām] al-Ḥusayn, and he concluded it with the Battle of al-Ḥarra. So the people abhorred him, and he was never blessed in his lifetime."[7]

On the other hand, if his admiration for this poetry stemmed from his love for Yazīd, this is enough to discredit the man. Loving Yazīd is the most substantial evidence of being a Nāṣibī and harboring hatred for the Ahl al-Bayt ﷺ. In this regard, Ibn Kathīr al-Damishqī provided ample evidence for this case when he said,

> "When it comes to Yazīd b. Mu'āwīya b. Abī Sufyān, people are divided into two groups; for some of them love him and are loyal followers to him, and these are a sect from the people of al-Shām, and they are Nawāsib."[8]

---

[7] Shams ad-Dīn adh-Dhahabī, *Siyār A'lām al-Nubalā'*, Vol. 4, p. 38.

[8] Ibn Kathīr, *al-Bidāya wa-l-Nihāya*, Vol. 6, p. 256.

Therefore, it is possible that some historians purposely differed in her naming, aiming to cast obscurity and doubt onto the cause, and Ibn Khallikān is merely an example of that.

Furthermore, the claim that her name is Maryam was solely propagated by al-Shahīd al-Awwal,[9] he reported this naming in a manner that indicates the narration is weak or doubtful (using the passive voice; e.g., it is said that...). I found no backup for this claim except for what al-Ḥusayn b. Ḥamdān al-Khaṣībī wrote,

> "It is said [regarding her naming]: Narjis, Sawsan, and Maryam the daughter of Zayd and sister of Ḥasan and Muḥammad b. Zayd, the preacher in Ṭabaristān, and the mix-up in naming occurred to the bondwoman mothers of children, and the most known and correct name is Narjis, so it is one of his indicators."[10]

Moreover, I could not find anyone who mentions that the preachers Ḥasan and Muḥammad in Ṭabaristān had a sister in the first place, so I cannot find evidence of a marriage or even a book of ancestry. So, think of it in any way you like; the truth remains that we cannot prove the existence of this person, let alone her marriage to Imām Ḥasan al-ʿAskarī ؑ!

---

[9] Shahīd al-Awwal, Muḥammad al-Shāmī al-ʿĀmilī al-Jizzīnī, *al-Durūs al-Sharʿiyyah fī Fiqh al-Imāmiyyah*, Vol. 2, p. 16.

[10] Khaṣībī, Ḥusayn b. Ḥamadān, *al-Hidāyat al-Kubrā*, p. 328.

This claim even contradicts many authentic and clear ḥadīths that we will later display on how Imām Muḥammad al-Mahdī ﷺ is the son of a bondmaid who is the lady of the bondmaids. The contrast here is that Maryam, the daughter of Zayd, is a free ʿAlawī woman, not a bondmaid, thus highlighting an apparent conflict in both groups.

Even if there were no conflict in what is presented, we cannot accept this claim as it is solely propagated by al-Ḥusayn b. Ḥamdān al-Khaṣībī, the leader of al-Nuṣayrīyah in his time, and whom al-Najashī ﵀ discussed as follows:

> "al-Ḥusayn b. Ḥamdān al-Khaṣībī al-Junbalānī Abū ʿAbdullāh was corrupt. Among his books are *Kitāb al-Ikhwān*, *Kitāb al-Masāʾil*, *Kitāb Tārīkh al-Aʾimmah*, and *Kitāb al-Risālah Takhlīṭ.*"[11]

Furthermore, the name "Malīka" is only found in one narration reported by Shaykh Muḥammad b. ʿAlī Ṣadūq ﵀, where the mother of Imām Muḥammad al-Mahdī introduced herself ﵁ by saying,

> "I am Malīka, the daughter of Yashua (Joshua) b. Caesar, the king of the Romans."[12]

---

[11] Ibn an-Nadīm, *Kitāb al-Fihrist*, p. 67.

[12] Ṣadūq, Shaykh Muḥammad b. ʿAlī, *Kamāl al-Dīn wa Tamām al-Niʿma*, p. 420.

The validity of this name thus falls upon the validity of this information; hence, the inauthenticity of this information mandates that this naming is not authentic.

Accordingly, most of these names need to be better established, thus narrowing down this circle of dispute, assuming a genuine dispute exists in the first place.

## Are These Names or Nicknames?

Another doubt is that these multiple names could not constitute actual first names; the narrators and historians have mixed up names and titles. According to linguists, the name is what man is first called, and the title or nickname is what he is known as for elevation [of status] or the opposite.

Looking at what have been termed as names, they may be nicknames as Sawsan, Rayḥāna, and Narjis, which are all names of flowers and plants that are known for their beauty or scent, and this suits the idea that these names are nicknames for her. Furthermore, there is a clear indicator that some of these are indeed nicknames, as Shaykh Muḥammad b. ʿAlī Ṣadūq ﷺ reported a narration on the secret behind calling her Ṣāqīl:

> "It is said: Sawsan; however, it is [also] said: Ṣāqīl due to [her] pregnancy."[13]

[13] Ibid., p. 432.

As such, citing multiple names for her is okay if we acknowledge that she has one name and multiple nicknames instead. One person can only have one name, but it is acceptable to have multiple titles. If you were to read biographies, you would notice that this is a widespread phenomenon among people. Hence, the high possibility that she has one single and a group of nicknames is viable to consider.

## Chastity of the 'Alawī Household

Another matter must be taken into account: the 'Alawī household was known for the chastity of its women and the intense jealousy of its men over the women. Therefore, it is unlikely that the men of this house would share many details about their women to the public.

That is why there is much dispute in the common knowledge about the wives of the infallible ﷺ and their daughters and the mixup in their names and biographies. For instance, historians are known to mix up between Zaynab al-Kubra and Umm Kulthūm, the daughters of Amīr al-Mu'minīn ؑ, and another case of such a mixup is the dispute regarding the daughters named Fātimah of Imām al-Ḥusayn ؑ, their number, and other significant differences in matters related to them.

Furthermore, the information on the name of Imām Muḥammad al-Mahdī's mother ؑ is reported from men outside the 'Alawī household who we are sure only specify the name of the Imām's mother 🕊 based on a guess, not certainty, and conjecture, not perception.

This is further evident in the mixup that occurred in some of what has been reported about several figures in Imām Ḥasan al-ʿAskarī's 🕊 household—for instance, Shaykh Muḥammad b. ʿAlī (Ibn Bābawayh) Ṣadūq 🕊 reported a story on the authority of Abī ʿAlī al-Khayzarānī about a bondmaid of his whom he had given to Abū Muḥammad (Imām Ḥasan) 🕊; when Jaʿfar al-Kadhāb [i.e., the liar] raided the house, she escaped back to him [from Jaʿfar], and he thus married her. Abū ʿAlī then said:

> "She told me that she had attended the birth of the Master 🕊, that his mother is called Ṣāqīl, and that Abū Muḥammad 🕊 had told her [Ṣāqīl] about what was happening to his children, so she asked to him to invoke God 🕊 to make it so that she meets her death before him. Thus, she died in the lifetime of Abī Muḥammad 🕊, and on her grave, there is a slab upon which 'this is the grave of Umm Muḥammad' is written."[14]

Undoubtedly, the bondmaid that is mentioned here is not Imām Muḥammad al-Mahdī's mother 🕊; instead, she is another woman who was probably in the house of Imām Ḥasan al-ʿAskarī 🕊, and proof of this is the consensus of historians on that the mother of Imām Muḥammad al-

---

14 Ṣadūq, Shaykh Muḥammad b. ʿAlī, *Kamāl al-Dīn wa Tamām al-Niʿma*, p. 431.

Mahdī died after Imām Ḥasan al-ʿAskarī ﷺ, and not before him, as we shall discuss later in more detail.

Therefore, all names attributed to the mother of Imām Muḥammad al-Mahdī that are not traced back to someone belonging to the ʿAlawī household remain a matter of doubt and dispute.

## Intentional Concealment

Another possibility is that the dispute on her naming stems from intentional concealment by Imām Ḥasan al-ʿAskarī ﷺ and the rest of the ʿAlawī household ﷺ in order to protect and safeguard Imām Muḥammad al-Mahdī ﷺ from the deceit of enemies. Just as the pregnancy was hidden and his birth was concealed—and it was even forbidden to utter his noble name in that period according to authentic texts—it is also possible that his mother ﷺ was also disguised and that the ʿAlawī household meant to produce this ambiguity in her regard so that the public is confused, thus disabling the government from using her as a means to pressure Imām Ḥasan al-ʿAskarī ﷺ.

Sayyid Muḥammad al-Ṣadr ﷺ suggested this possibility in his encyclopedia as follows: She (may God be pleased with her) had followed a special plan in switching up her name now and then and using several names at the same time and at different times. She lived in this way ever since she joined this noble family because she was to be the mother of Imām al-Mahdī ﷺ and was thus prone to be persecuted and hunted by the authorities and imprisoned for a time. Hence, this plan was put in place as a precaution and as safety to protect her and her son and to confuse the authorities as to which one of these names [identities] is the one to be imprisoned, or the one who is pregnant, or the one who is the mother, and so on... The authorities would then think that these names belong to several women and would thus neglect the possibility of one woman holding all these names, and this is the third possibility that is likely possible in the case of the mother of Imām al-Mahdī ﷿.[15]

Perhaps this is also what al-Nūrī ﷫ meant when he reported the following information that proves that she had multiple names:

"The narrator then asked him about the mother of the Imām ﷺ, and he said: His mother is Malīka who is some days called Sawsan and other days Rayḥāna, and Ṣāqīl and Narjis were among her names as well. As such, the conflict in her naming ﷺ is apparent as she was referred to with all these five names."[16]

It is truly astonishing how someone could enforce on the Shī'a such a [meaningless] dispute and consider it a

---

[15] Ṣadr, Sayyid Muḥammad Muḥammad Ṣādiq, *Mawsu'at al-Imām al-Mahdī* ﷺ, Vol. 1, p. 244.

[16] Ṭabrisī, Mīrzā Ḥusayn Nūrī, *al-Najm al-Thāqib fī Aḥwāl al-Ḥujjah al-Ghā'ib*, Vol. 1, p. 135.

contradiction and a discredit to the Mahdīst ideology, neglecting that this dispute is present in their books in a way that is much greater and more severe than what was aforementioned:

The most major narrator of the books of Ahl al-Sunnah wal-Jamāʿah is Abū Hurayrah. According to statistics by Ibn Ḥazm al-Ẓāhirī, Abū Hurayrah reported a total of 5374 ḥadīths,[17] yet there was a severe dispute on his name as al-Nawawī said:

> "The ḥadīth narrator Abū Hurayrah ﷺ was the first to be given this nickname. He had a cat he used to play with when he was young, so he was nicknamed as such ["Hurayrah" means kitten in Arabic]. There was much dispute in his and his father's [real] names; the most famous and authentic of his names was ʿAbd al-Rahman b. Sakhr and many people in this field assert the same."[18]

Ibn ʿAbd al-Bar said:

> "People differed greatly on the actual names of Abī Hurayrah and his father, and this dispute could not be settled in the pre-Islamic or Islamic era.

[17] al-Andalusī, ʿAlī b. Aḥmad b. Ḥazm, *Jawāmiʿ al-Sīrah wa Khams Rasāʾil Ukhra*, p. 275.

[18] *al-Majmūʿ*, Vol. 1, p. 266.

Khalifa said that Abī Hurayrah's name is said to be Ibn ʿAmir, Bārīr b. Ashraqah, and Sākīn b. Dumah.

Aḥmad b. Ẓuhayr said he had heard his father say Abī Hurayrah's name is ʿAbdullāh b. ʿAbd Shams, and it is also said to be ʿAmir, and he said:

> I heard Aḥmad b. Ḥanbal say that Abī Hurayrah's name is "Abdullāh b. ʿAbd Shams and it is also said ʿAbd Naḥm b. ʿAmir, ʿAbd Ghannām, and Sākīn.

Furthermore, Zakar Muḥammad b. Yaḥyā al-Zahalī reports on the authority of Aḥmad b. Ḥanbal the same, and ʿAbbās said that he heard Yaḥyā b. Muʿīn say that Abī Hurayrah's name is ʿAbd Shams.

Similarly, Abū Naʿīm says that Abī Hurayrah's name is ʿAbd Shams.

Sufyān b. Ḥasīn narrated on the authority of al-Zuhrī, on the authority of al-Muḥarir b. Abī Hurayrah, the following:

> Abī Hurayrah's name is ʿAbd ʿAmrū b. ʿAbd Ghannām.

Abū Faḥs al-Fallas said:

> The most authentic information we know regarding the name of Abī Hurayrah is that it is ʿAbd ʿAmrū b. ʿAbd Ghannām.

Ibn Jārūd said Abī Hurayrah's name is Kardūs and al-Fāḍil b. Mūsā al-Ṣinānī narrated on the authority of Muḥammad b. ʿAmrū, on the authority of Abī Salma b. ʿAbd al-Raḥmān, that Abī Hurayrah [is called] ʿAbd Shams, from al-ʿAẓd, from Ḍūs.

Abū Ḥātim al-Rāzi mentioned on the authority of al-Awṣī, on the authority of Ibn Ḥalīʿa, that Abī Hurayrah's name is Kardūs b. ʿAmir.

Al-Bukhārī mentioned on the authority of Ibn Abī al-Aswad that Abī Hurayrah's name is ʿAbd Shams, and it is said ʿAbd Naḥm or ʿAbd ʿAmrū.

Abū ʿĀmir said that his name cannot be ʿAbd Shams, ʿAbd ʿAmrū, ʿAbd Ghannām, or ʿAbd Naḥm, and if any of these names is authentic, then it was so in the pre-Islamic era only; as for the Islamic era, his name is ʿAbdullāh or ʿAbd al-Raḥman, only God knows, for there is significant dispute in this regard as well."[19]

In conclusion, all the answers presented herein are sufficient to completely uproot the issue of the Shīʿa's dispute on the name of Imām Muḥammad al-Mahdī's ﷻ mother ﷺ, leaving no trace behind. Discussion only remains regarding what her authentic name is, and this cannot be concluded certainly due to the factors and possibilities presented previously. Nonetheless, we can say

[19] al-Andalusī, Ibn ʿAbd al-Barr, *al-Istīʿāb fī Maʿrifat al-Aṣḥāb*, Vol. 4, p. 1786.

that Narjis is highly likely to be the most authentic because it is most frequently mentioned in the narrations about them ﷺ.

Furthermore, the following is a text of utmost importance:

> "I read in the book of *al-Wasāya* and others that a congregation of scholars and wise men, including ʿAslān al-Kalābī, Mūsā b. Aḥmad al-Fazārī, and Aḥmad b. Jaʿfar and Muḥammad reported that Ḥakīmah the daughter of Abū Jaʿfar, the aunt of Abū Muḥammad ﷺ, used to pray to God to grace him [Abū Muḥammad] with a child, so he said to her:
>
> > Oh aunt, the newborn we were expecting will be born tonight, on the night of the middle of Shaʿbān in the year 255, so break your fast with us, and it was a Friday night.
>
> Ḥakīmah said:
>
> > Who is the mother of this newborn, my master?
>
> He replied:
>
> > Narjis."[20]

The report highlights the special name (Narjis) that she was called by within the ʿAlawī household, considering that the

[20] Ibn ʿAbd al-Wahhāb, Shaykh Ḥusayn, *ʿUyūn al-Muʿjizāt*, p. 128.

phrase "I read in the book of *al-Wasāya* and others" indicates that this report was widespread in the books of the companions. In this regard, the book above is sufficient to mention; *al-Wasāya* was authored by al-Shalmaghānī[21] who was killed in 322 AH and who was, during his days of righteousness, close with the deputies of the Imām of the Time ﷻ, and this is enough proof of what we suggested.

Our suggestion of this name does not imply the elimination of the possibility that all the other names are nicknames for her or that they were used to intentionally obscure her identity and protect her from the tyranny of the Sulṭān (as will be discussed in detail later), and it is entirely acceptable to combine all these possible answers.

---

[21] On p. 378 of *al-Fihrist*, al-Najashī said: Abū Ja'far, who is known as Ibn Abī al-Azaqīr, was among the forerunners of our companions, but his envy of Abī Qāsim al-Ḥusayn b. Rūḥ pushed him to reject and abandon the [Shī'a] sect and join other dreadful groups and sects until the Imām cursed him via a letter, and so, the Sulṭān at that time killed him and crucified him.

# Her Story

One of the most important matters related to Imām Muḥammad al-Mahdī's mother ﷺ is how she reached the infallible Ahl al-Bayt. This matter is linked to her origin and the truth of her identity, and it also requires authenticating and negating many other matters.

## The Account of Her Coming from the Land of the Romans

The most critical information in this regard is a narration reported by Shaykh Muḥammad b. 'Alī Ṣadūq ﷺ[22]. This report includes a detailed account of Imām Muḥammad al-Mahdī's mother ﷺ and all that is related to her life:

"Muḥammad b. 'Alī b. Ḥātim al-Nawfalī narrated to us: Abū al-'Abbās Aḥmad b. 'Īsā al-Washā' al-Baghdādī narrated to us: Aḥmad b. Ṭāhir al-Qummī narrated to us: Abū al-Ḥusayn Muḥammad b. Bahr al-Shaybānī narrated to us that he said:

> I came to Karbalā' in the year 286 AH and visited the tomb of the forlorn son of the Messenger of God ﷺ and then returned to Baghdād, intending to go to the cemetery of Qurayshī called Maqābir Qurayshī, the Shrine of the Kāẓimayn ﷺ. It was so hot that the noontime had been set ablaze, and the heavens were burning in flames.

[22] Ṣadūq, Shaykh Muḥammad b. 'Alī, *Kamāl al-Dīn wa Tamām al-Ni'ma*.

When I reached the shrine of Imām Mūsā al-Kāẓim ﷺ and smelled the breeze of his tomb that is engulfed in Divine compassion and encircled by gardens of forgiveness, my body shook with grievous sobs, and tears rolled down my face, blurring my vision. When my tears ceased, and my wailing stopped, and I opened my eyes, I saw an old man whose back was bent and his knees were curved, and his forehead and palms appeared as dry as the knees of a camel.

Near the tomb, he was saying to another gentleman who was with him:

> O nephew, through the most esoteric secrets and the noblest of all knowledge, which the two Masters possess, your uncle has reached a nobility the likes of which none has carried but Salmān. Your uncle has reached the end of his life, yet he does not find in the people of the locality a man to confide his knowledge in.

I said to myself:

> Oh my soul, hardship and suffering befall you since I exhaust the foot and the hoof in search of knowledge. Now, my ears have caught from this old man a word which alludes to the greatest knowledge and a magnificent affair.

I asked the old gentleman:

> O Shaykh, who are the two Masters?

He replied:

> The Two Heavenly Stars treasured on Earth in *Ṣurrah Man Ra'ā* [i.e., today known as Sammara].

I said:

> I take an oath by the love and the majestic status of Imāmate and succession of these two Masters that I am a searcher of their knowledge and a seeker of their words. I profess the solemnest of oaths to protect their secrets.

He said:

> If you are truthful in what you are saying, then present the words from the narrators of their traditions.

He looked through the books, examined the traditions, and said:

> You are truthful. I am Bishr b. Sulaymān al-Nakhās from the progeny of Abū Ayyūb al-Ansārī, one of the devotees of Abū al-Ḥasan and Abū Muḥammad ﷺ and their neighbor at Ṣurrah Man Ra'ā.

I told him,

> Favor me by sharing some of the things you have seen from them.

He said [the following quote is all narrated by Bishr until the closing quote]:

> My master Abū al-Ḥasan [Imām ʿAlī al-Hādī] عليه السلام taught me about the matter of slaves. I would buy and sell only with his permission, which helped me avoid dubious occasions until my knowledge of the subject matured. I could better distinguish between the permissible and the forbidden. As such, one night, I was at my house in Ṣurrah Man Raʾā, and some hours had passed when someone knocked at my door. I hurried over and saw Kāfūr, the servant, the messenger of our Master, Abū al-Ḥasan ʿAlī b. Muḥammad [Imām ʿAlī al-Hādī] عليه السلام, calling me to him. I got dressed and went to him. I saw him talking to his son, Abū Muḥammad [Imām Ḥasan al-ʿAskarī] عليه السلام, and his sister, Ḥakīmah, from behind the curtain.
>
> When I sat, he said:
>
> > O Bishr, you are from the descendants of the Anṣār, and this love has always been steadfast in you, with each coming generation inheriting it from the preceding one, and you are

> trustworthy men of us, Ahl al-Bayt ﷺ. I am elevating you and ennobling you with an excellence that will surpass all Shīʿa in devotion by sharing a secret with you and sending you to purchase a certain bondmaid. He then wrote an excellent letter in Roman script and Roman language and imprinted his seal.

He took out a yellow cloth that held 200 dinars and instructed me the following:

> Take this and go to Baghdād, to the crossing of the Euphrates on the noon of such and such day. When you reach the boats of the captives, you will see bondmaids in them. You will find buyers for the procurers of the ʿAbbāsids and a small group of Arab youths. When you see that, watch for a man called ʿUmar b. Yazīd al-Nakhās from a distance all day until a bondmaid of certain traits is brought to the buyers. She is dressed in two thick silks; she refuses to be seen or touched by the examiners; she does not submit to anyone who wants to touch her and gaze at her from behind the thin veil, and al-Nakhās will strike her, and she shall yell in Romanian.
>
> So, you should know that she is saying,
>
> Alas, from the violation of the veil.

One of the buyers says:

> She shall be mine for 300 dinars; her modesty has increased my desire for her.

She replies to him in Arabic:

> Even if you come in the attire of Sulaymān (Solomon), the son of Dāwūd (David), with a kingdom like his, I will not be interested in you. So, save your money.

The slave-dealer al-Nakhās says:

> Then what is the solution? I have to sell you.

The bondmaid replies:

> What is the rush? There must be a buyer who soothes my heart and offers me his fidelity and honesty.

[I was told] at this moment, you must go to 'Umar b. Yazīd al-Nakhās and tell him the following:

> I have a sealed letter from a man of nobility, which he has written in the Roman language and the Roman script. The letter describes his benevolence, fidelity,

> excellence, and generosity, so give her the letter so that she may discern from it the character of its author. Should she be interested in him and choose him, I am his representative in buying her from you.

I performed all that my Master, Abū Muḥammad al-Ḥasan [Imām Ḥasan al-ʿAskarī] عليه السلام, had ordered me to do concerning the bondmaid. When she saw the epistle, she cried profusely and told ʿUmar b. Yazīd to sell her to the writer of this letter. She took the solemnest of oaths that if he were to refuse to sell her to him, she would kill herself.

I negotiated the price with the dealer until it settled precisely on the amount of dinars my Master عليه السلام had given me in the yellow cloth. Once he took the money from me, I received the bondmaid, who was brimming with joy and laughter. I returned with her to the quarters I was residing at in Baghdād. She was very restless until she took out the letter of our Master from her pocket, kissed it, put it on her eyes and cheeks, and touched it to her body.

Astonished by this, I said:

> You are kissing a letter whose author you do not know!

She said:

> O you weak person with a lack of knowledge on the status of the progeny of prophets, lend me your ears and empty your heart for my words. I am Malīka, the daughter of Yashua, son of Caesar, the king of Rome. My mother is from the descendants of the Disciples of 'Īsā [the Ḥawāriyyūn], and her lineage goes back to the successor of 'Īsā, Sham'ūn. I will tell you a wondrous story. My grandfather, Caesar, wanted to marry me to his nephew when I was a 13-year-old girl. So he gathered 300 priests and monks in his palace from the descendants of the Ḥawāriyyūn and their men of stature seven hundred men. He gathered four thousand men from the army commanders, military officers, armed forces leaders, and chiefs of the tribes. He erected a throne from the dearest of his riches, adorned with varieties of jewels, and raised over forty steps. When his nephew climbed up, the crosses were fixed about, the bishops took their stands in great reverence, and the pages of the Gospel were opened. Suddenly, the crosses fell to the ground, and the pillars of the throne crumbled and crashed onto the floor. My grandfather's nephew, who had

risen over the throne, fell unconscious. The bishops' faces lost their colors, and their chests shook. Their leader said to my grandfather:

> Please excuse me from facing this evil that forebodes the demise of this Christian religion and the regal creed.

My grandfather took this as an evil omen and said to the bishops:

> Erect these scaffolds and raise the crosses and bring the brother of this deceased man, whose dreams have been ruined, so I may marry him to this young girl such that the evil of his dead brother may be warded through his fortune.

However, the second nephew suffered the same fate as the first. People scrambled away. My grandfather, the Caesar, got up in great distress and hurried into his palace. I dropped the curtains; during that same night, I saw in my dream that ʿĪsā, Shamʿūn, and a number of the Ḥawāriyyūn had gathered at my grandfather's palace and had erected there a pulpit that defied the Heavens in height and elevation; it was situated in the same spot where my grandfather had installed his throne. At this moment, [Prophet] Muḥammad ﷺ, accompanied by some young men and some of his sons, entered upon them. ʿĪsā stepped toward him and embraced him.

The Prophet said to him:

> O Spirit of God, I have come to you to propose a marriage between the daughter, Malīka, of your successor Shamʿūn and this son of mine. As he was saying this, he pointed to his son Abū Muḥammad ؑ, the writer of this epistle.

ʿĪsā looked at Shamʿūn and said to him:

> The most incredible honor has come to you; so form a kinship between your house and the house of Muḥammad ﷺ.

Shamʿūn said:

> Indeed, I shall do so. He then climbed up the pulpit. Muḥammad ﷺ said the rituals and married me to his son while

> ʿĪsā ﷺ, the sons of Muḥammad ﷺ, and the Ḥawāriyyūn bore witness.

When I woke up, I was scared to tell my father or grandfather about this dream, fearing that they would kill me. So I kept it a secret from them while my heart throbbed with love for Abū Muḥammad ﷺ so much that I forsook eating and drinking. Thus, I grew weak; my body became thin and frail, and I fell severely ill. My grandfather summoned every physician from the cities of Rome to treat me, but to no avail.

When he was overcome with despair, he said to me:

> O solace of my heart, do you have any such desire or wish so that I may fulfill it?

I said:

> Grandfather, I feel no relief in sight. However, if you spare the Muslims in your prison from torture, remove their manacles, do good to them, and kindly release them, then I am hopeful that ʿĪsā and his mother will give me health.

I tried to look healthier when he did that and ate a little food. This made him very happy, and he became enthused to respect and be kind to the captives. After four nights, I also saw [in the realm of dreams] the Mistress of the women of the worlds, Lady Fāṭimah 🌸. She visited me along with Mary, the daughter of 'Imrān (Amram), and one thousand serfs from the Gardens.

Mary tells me:

> This is the Mistress of the Ladies, the mother of your husband, Abū Muḥammad 🌸 [Imām Ḥasan al-'Askarī 🌸].

So I clung to her, crying and complaining about why Abū Muḥammad 🌸 had not visited me.

So the Mistress of the Ladies 🌸 said:

> My son, Abū Muḥammad, will not visit you as long as you associate a partner to God and believe in the religion of the Christians. My sister Mary has turned to God with disdain from your religion. If you want to

> please God, the Mighty, the Sublime, and ʿĪsā and his mother, and if you want Abū Muḥammad عليه السلام to visit you, then say:
>
> > I bear witness that there is no deity but God and that Muḥammad—my father—is the Messenger of God.

When I uttered these words, the Mistress of the Ladies عليها السلام embraced me, and my soul was blessed.

She said:

> Now expect a visit from Abū Muḥammad; I am sending him to you. I was excited and yearning to meet Abū Muḥammad when I woke up.

The next night, Abū Muḥammad visited me in my dream, and it was as if I was saying to him:

> You have abandoned me, my beloved, while your love fully occupied my heart.

He said:

> My delay was not but for your polytheistic belief. Now that you have embraced Islam,

> I am going to visit you every night until God unites us. To this moment, his visits to me have not yet ceased.

So I [Bishr] asked her:

> How did you fall among the captives?

She said:

> One night, Abū Muḥammad ﷺ told me that my grandfather will shortly be dispatching an army to fight the Muslims on such and such day and that he will follow them, so I must join them disguised as a servant among the entourage of the servants along such and such route. I did as he said, and the vanguards of Muslims encountered us, which led to my situation, as you can see, with no one aware that I am the granddaughter of the king of the Romans until now except for you, and that is because I told you. The man in whose share of booty I fell asked me for my name. I hid my identity from him and said:
>
> Narjis.

He said:

> A name of servants.

So I [Bishr] said to her:

> It is astonishing that you are Roman, yet your language is Arabic.

To this, she replied:

> My grandfather was persistent and always encouraged me to advance my learning, so he appointed a woman, who was his translator, to visit me. She would come to me day and night and teach me Arabic until I became fluent and articulate.

Bishr continued, and he said:

> When I brought her back to Ṣurrah Man Raʾā, I came to our Master Abū al-Ḥasan [Imām ʿAlī al-Hādī] عليه السلام.

He asked her:

> How did God show you the glory of Islam, the disgrace of Christianity, and the nobility of Muḥammad ﷺ and his Household عليهم السلام?

So she said:

> How can I describe, O son of God's Messenger, something that you know better than me?

He said:

> I want to honor you. Which one is dearer to you: ten thousand dinars or a glad tiding to you of eternal grandeur?

She said:

> Indeed, glad tidings!

He ؑ said:

> So rejoice the tidings of bearing a son who will rule the world from the east to the west and fill the Earth with justice and equity as it was filled with oppression and corruption.

She asked:

> From whom?

He replied in Roman:

> From whom did the Messenger of God ﷺ propose for you on such and such night, in such a year?

She said:

> From ʿĪsā and his successor.

So he asked:

> And to whom did ʿĪsā and his successor marry you?

She said:

> From your son Abū Muḥammad.

He asked:

> Do you know him?

To which she replied:

> How could I not when he has been visiting me every night since I embraced Islam at the hands of the Mistress of the Ladies, his mother?

So Abū al-Ḥasan [Imām ʿAlī al-Hādī] ﷺ said:

> Kāfūr, call my sister Ḥakīmah.

And when she came, he said to her:

> Here she is.

Lady Ḥakīmah was elated to see her and embraced her long and tight.

So our Master told her:

> O daughter of the Messenger of God, take her to your house and teach her the duties and traditions, for she is the wife of Abū Muḥammad and the mother of the Qāʾim عجل الله تعالى فرجه الشريف."

This account was reported by the following who came after Shaykh Muḥammad b. ʿAlī Ṣadūq:

- Shaykh Muḥammad b. Ḥasan Ṭūsī قدس سره[23]
- Muḥammad b. Jarīr al-Ṭabarī قدس سره[24]

---

[23] Ṭūsī, Shaykh Muḥammad b. Ḥasan, *Kitāb al-Ghaybah*, p. 208.

[24] al-Ṭabarī, Muḥammad b. Jarīr, *Dalāʾil al-Imāmat*, p. 489.

- Muḥammad b. Ḥasan al-Fattāl al-Nayshābūrī رحمه الله[25]

- Muḥammad b. ʿAlī b. Shahrāshūb رحمه الله[26]

Hence, since the time of al-Ṣadūq رحمه الله, this account has become the official story of Imām Muḥammad al-Mahdī's عجل الله تعالى فرجه الشريف mother عليها السلام, thus necessitating much research and investigation into its fine details.

## A Look into the Chain of Narrators [Sanad]

When considering the chain of narrators [or chain of transmission] of this report, we find some issues therein, and they are as follows:

First: The narrator of this account is Abū al-Ḥusayn Muḥammad b. Bahr al-Shaybānī. Regardless of our evaluation of this man at the moment, it is extraordinary that Shaykh Muḥammad b. ʿAlī Ṣadūq, who died in 381 AH, reported this account on his authority via three transmitters: ("Muḥammad b. ʿAlī b. Hātim al-Nawfalī narrated to us: Abū al-ʿAbbās Aḥmad b. ʿĪsā al-Washāʾ al-Baghdādī narrated to us: Aḥmad b. Ṭāhir al-Qummī narrated to us:..."); on the other hand, we find that Shaykh Muḥammad b. Ḥasan Ṭūsī, who was born in 385 AH and

---

[25] Nayshābūrī, Muḥammad b. Ḥasan al-Fattāl, *Rawḍat al-Wāʿiẓīn wa Baṣīrat al-Muttaʿiẓīn*, p. 252.

[26] Ibn Shahrāshūb, Muḥammad b. ʿAlī, *Manāqib Āl Abī Ṭālib*, Vol. 3, p. 538.

died in 460 AH, reported this same account on his authority but via two transmitters only:

> "A group of people told me on the authority of Abū al-Mufaḍḍal al-Shaybānī...)!"[27]

Even stranger is what Muḥammad b. Jarīr al-Ṭabarī reported:

> "Abū al-Mufaḍḍal Muḥammad b. 'Abdullāh b. al-Muṭṭalib al-Shaybānī narrated to us in the year 385: Abū al-Ḥusayn Muḥammad b. Bahr al-Raḥnī al-Shaybānī narrated to us: I came to Karbalā' in the year 286..."[28]

From this, we infer that the meeting happened in 286 AH, yet the person involved talked about it in 385 AH, 100 years later.

This significant time gap reinforces that there are missing transmitters in the chain of narrators that Shaykh Muḥammad b. Ḥasan Ṭūsī and al-Ṭabarī al-Saghir ﷺ reported. As such, it appears that the account and chain of narrators reported by Shaykh Muḥammad b. 'Alī Ṣadūq is the most accurate and authentic.

---

[27] Ṭūsī, Shaykh Muḥammad b. Ḥasan, *al-Ghaybah*, p. 208.

[28] al-Ṭabarī, Muḥammad b. Jarīr, *Dalā'il al-Imāmat*, p. 489.

Herein lies an issue: we do not know the identity of those who transmitted this story under the authority of Muḥammad b. Bahr al-Shaybānī—even those whom Shaykh Muḥammad b. ʿAlī Ṣadūq mentioned in the chain of narrators or chain of transmission [sanad] (Aḥmad b. ʿĪsā al-Washā', Aḥmad b. Ṭāhir al-Qummī) are overlooked in *Kitāb al-Rijāl* [a book that studies reporters of ḥadīth] and biographies, and there are no biographies on them or documents that identify them. Thus, the chain of narrators leading up to the originator of the story is either "ḍaʿīf" [weak] due to the presence of unknown transmitters in its chain or "mursal" [transmitted or sent] due to missing or unknown transmitters.

Second: This account revolved around Bishr b. Sulaymān al-Nakhās, who introduced himself in the narration that he is from the progeny of Abī Ayyūb al-Ansārī; however, there is no mention of this man in history books, *al-Rijāl*, or biographies. Even the narrator of this report (Muḥammad b. Bahr al-Shaybānī) did not know him and had not heard of him before. Instead, he only got to know him and believed his words after the man introduced himself. So, we have no way of knowing this man except how he introduced himself in this narration!

What is even stranger is how he described himself with grandiosity, saying the following:

> "O nephew, through the most esoteric secrets and the noblest of all knowledge, which the two Masters

possess, your uncle has reached a nobility the likes of which none has carried but Salmān."

Is it possible that there be a companion of the Imāms ☝, like Salmān al-Muḥammadi, yet no one knows anything about him? Furthermore, it is also noteworthy that he introduced him as a descendent of Abū Ayyūb al-Ansārī, where he said:

"You are truthful. I am Bishr b. Sulaymān al-Nakhās from the progeny of Abū Ayyūb al-Ansārī."

However, historians reported that Abū Ayyūb had no offspring; Ibn As'ad said that Abū Ayyūb had a son named 'Abd al-Rahman—his mother was Umm Ḥasan, the daughter of Zayd b. Thābit b. al-Ḍaḥḥāk from Banī Mālik b. al-Najjār—but his son vanished, so I do not know his descendants.[29]

Therefore, the authenticity of this account hinges upon how much we know and believe this figure. Moreover, that is based on the assumption that the story's narrator is truthful; otherwise, this figure may be entirely fictional and imagined, wrongly spread among the people.

Third: Now, we examine the primary source of the account. Reviewing the books of narration, we find that this story is transmitted in two ways:

---

[29] al-Baghdādī, Muḥammad b. Sa'ad b. Manī', *al-Ṭabaqāt al-Kubrā*, Vol. 3, p. 484.

1. The chain of narrators reported by Shaykh Muḥammad b. ʿAlī Ṣadūq 📿:

> "Muḥammad b. ʿAlī b. Ḥātim al-Nawfalī narrated to us: Abū al-ʿAbbās Aḥmad b. ʿĪsā al-Washāʾ al-Baghdādī narrated to us: Aḥmad b. Ṭāhir al-Qummī narrated to us: Abū al-Ḥusayn Muḥammad b. Bahr al-Shaybānī narrated to us that he said:...".[30]

2. The chain of narrators reported by Shaykh Muḥammad b. Ḥasan Ṭūsī 📿:

> "A group of people reported on the authority of Abū al-Mufaḍḍal al-Shaybānī, on the authority of Abū al-Ḥusayn Muḥammad b. Bahr b. Sahl al-Shaybānī al-Raḥnī...".[31]

In both ways, there is one common narrator (Muḥammad b. Bahr al-Raḥnī). Shaykh Muḥammad b. ʿAlī Ṣadūq had also reported another narration on his authority:

> "Muḥammad b. Ḥātim al-Nawfalī, known as al-Karmānī, narrated Abū al-ʿAbbās Aḥmad b. ʿĪsā al-Washāʾ al-Baghdādī narrated to us: Aḥmad b. Ṭāhir al-Qummī narrated to us: Muḥammad b. Bahr b. Sahl al-

---

[30] Ṣadūq, Shaykh Muḥammad b. ʿAlī, *Kamāl al-Dīn wa Tamām al-Niʿma*, p. 417.

[31] Ṭūsī, Shaykh Muḥammad b. Ḥasan, *al-Ghaybah*, p. 208.

> Shaybānī narrated to us: 'Alī b. al-Ḥārith, on the authority of Sā'īd b. Manṣūr al-Jawshanī narrated to us that Aḥmad b. 'Alī al-Badīlī said: My father told us on the authority of Sudayr al-Sayrafī: al-Mufaḍḍal b. 'Umar and I entered...".[32]

Shaykh Muḥammad b. Ḥasan Ṭūsī reported this same narration as well using the first chain of narrators [sanad] we mentioned earlier:

> "A group of people told me on the authority of Abū al-Mufaḍḍal Muḥammad b. 'Abdullāh b. Muḥammad b. 'Ubaydullāh b. al-Muṭṭalib ﵀ that he said: Abū al-Ḥusayn Muḥammad b. Bahr b. Sahl al-Shaybānī al-Jawshanī told us: Aḥmad b. 'Alī al-Badilī told us: My father told me on the authority of Sudayr al-Sayrafī: al-Mufaḍḍal b. 'Umar and I entered...".[33]

As such, it is prudent to investigate this man around which this narration revolves, as he is the only one to have met "Bishr al-Nakhas" and got to know what occurred between him and the two Imāms ﵉ and the pure Lady Narjis ﵍.

---

[32] Ṣadūq, Shaykh Muḥammad b. 'Alī, *Kamāl al-Dīn wa Tamām al-Ni'ma*, p. 352.

[33] Ṭūsī, Shaykh Muḥammad b. Ḥasan, *al-Ghaybah*, p. 208.

Al-Najashī said,

> "Muḥammad b. Bahr al-Raḥnī Abū al-Ḥusayn al-Shaybānī was a resident of Narmashīr in the land of Kermān. Some of our companions stated that he exaggerated his beliefs [ghulūw]; however, I do not know the reason behind these claims as his narrations appear decent. He also authored books, including *Kitāb al-Bidā'*, *Kitāb al-Biqā'*, *Kitāb al-Taqwā*, *Kitāb al-Ittibā' wa-Tark al-Murā'a fī al-Qur'ān*. *Kitāb al-Burhān*, *Kitāb al-Awwal wa al-Ashrā'*, *Kitāb al-Mut'ah*, and *Kitāb al-Qalā'id* dealing with many issues of conflict between the transgressors and us. Abū al-'Abbās Aḥmad b. 'Alī b. al-'Abbās b. Nūḥ said to us: Muḥammad b. Bahr told us about all his books and narrations."[34]

The Shaykh's words are a testimony that he was accused of exaggeration [ghulūw] by some companions, and by "some companions"; perhaps the Shaykh is referring to Ibn al-Ghadā'irī who said about him [Muḥammad b. Bahr]: His beliefs are weakened by his exaggeration [ghulūw].[35] However, the Shaykh ﵀ came to his defense by saying,

> "...however, I do not know the reason behind these claims as his narrations appear to be decent."

---

[34] al-Najāshī, Aḥmad, *al-Fihrist*, p. 384.

[35] al-Ḥillī, 'Allāmah Ḥasan, *Khulāṣat al-Aqwāl fī Ma'rifat al-Rijāl*, p. 397.

Some concluded al-Najashī's approval of this man's authenticity through this statement. However, some issues can be raised in this regard:

First, al-Najashī's ﵀ defense of al-Raḥnī is based on conjecture only. The phrase "his narrations appear to be decent" indicates that his refusal to accuse the man with ghulūw is inferred from his evaluation of his narrations and not from directly interacting with the man or the people who know him personally.

Second, It seems that the books of al-Raḥnī were not widespread in Baghdād, and proof of this is what Shaykh Muḥammad b. Ḥasan Ṭūsī ﵀ said:

> "He has authored around 500 works and letters, and most of his books are present in Khurāsān."[36]

In turn, this leads us to doubt whether al-Najashī could examine the man's legacy for him to deem him innocent of what he has been accused of.

Third: In our hands is a tangible testimony that reveals the truth of this man, and it is what al-Kashshī ﵀ mentioned in his *al-Rijāl*:

> "Abū ʿUmar and Muḥammad b. ʿUmar b. ʿAbdulʿazīz al-Kashshī said: Abū al-Ḥasan Muḥammad b. Bahr al-

[36] Ṭūsī, Shaykh Muḥammad b. Ḥasan, *al-Fihrist*, p. 208.

> Karmānī al-Raḥnī al-Tarmashīrī told me that he was among the extremist Ghulāt."[37]

Furthermore, in another source, al-Kashshī said:

> "Muḥammad b. Bahr is a Ghālī [one who exaggerates in his beliefs; i.e., one who practices ghulūw], Faḍlullāh is not one of Jacob's men, and this ḥadīth has been added to in a way that changes his face."[38]

This testimony is an important indicator that proves that the man is a Ghālī, an extremist one at that, too, as per al-Kashshī's ﵀ words; more importantly, his words also suggest that the man enjoyed manipulating narrations, adding and omitting from them as he pleased.

Furthermore, another text reinforces what we have presented thus far about the man. It is what Yāqūt al-Ḥamawī reported on the authority of Ibn Shahr Āshūb, ﵀:

> "He used to memorize and teacher eight thousand narrations, and he would show interest in strange reports; he who follows the strangest of narrations surely lies."[39]

---

[37] Ṭūsī, Shaykh Muḥammad b. Ḥasan, *Ikhtīyār Ma'rifat al-Rijāl*, Vol. 1, p. 362.

[38] Ibid., p. 363.

[39] al-Ḥamawī, Yāqūt, *Mu'jam al-Udabā'*, Vol. 18, p. 31.

This testimony carries a tangible reality that is possible to realize by examining and evaluating the narrations reported by this man. In this regard, the narrations that we have from Muḥammad b. Bahr al-Raḥnī is a matter of conflict and confusion. Al-Kāshī 🕮 reported one of his narrations, and it is as follows:

"Abū 'Abdillah 🕮 was told:

> Zurārah claimed to have taken power from you.

He said:

> May they suffer in what I shall do to them, this renegade was between my hands, and I had shown him while he was blind between the Heavens and the Earth, but he doubted and thought I was a magician.

So I said:

> O God, if Hell were not so small, then it would have contained the house of 'Uyūn b. Ṣanṣān.

It was said:

> [What about] Ḥimrān?

He said:

> Ḥimrān is not among them."[40]

This narration is false, for it not only contains strong criticism of great companions of the Imāms ﷺ (Abī Basīr al-Marādī and house of 'Uyūn) but also testifies that they belong to Hell!

Furthermore, Shaykh Muḥammad b. 'Alī Ṣadūq ﷺ, extracted long texts from al-Raḥnī's book *Min Qawl Mufaḍḍilu al-Anbiyā' wal-Rusul wal-A'immah wal-Ḥujaj Ṣalawāt Allāh 'Alayhim Ajma'īn 'Alā al-Malā'ikah* and he commented on them in a way that indicates his disapproval in the man's narrations. He said:

> "The compiler of this book said: I wanted this story to be in this book, and regarding Iblīs, I say that he was not that he was one of the angels, but instead he was one of the jinn, except that he worshiped God among the angels, and Hārūt and Mārūt are two angels, and my saying about them is not what the people of the Ḥashw [a deviant sect of anthropomorphists] say; instead, I believe they were infallible.

[40] Ṭūsī, Shaykh Muḥammad b. Ḥasan, *Ikhtīyār Ma'rifat al-Rijāl*, Vol. 1, p. 372.

The verse:

﴿وَاتَّبَعوا ما تَتلو الشَّياطينُ عَلى مُلكِ سُلَيمانَ﴾

﴿*wa-ttaba'ū mā tatlū sh-shayāṭīnu 'alā mulki sulaymāna wa-mā kafara sulaymānu*﴾

﴿*And they followed what the devils pursued during Sulaymān's reign**﴾[41]

means that they followed what the devils recited to King Sulaymān and to what was revealed to the two angels in Babylon, Hārūt and Mārūt, and I ascertained a supporting report about that in the book *'Uyūn Akhbār al-Riḍā* ﷺ'"[42]

His words are clear indicators that the man belongs to the Ḥashwiyyah [a deviant sect of anthropomorphists] and that what he reported contradicts the narrations attributed to the Ahl al-Bayt ﷺ.

---

[41] Sūrat al-Baqarah, Verse 102.

* Or 'they followed what the devils recited during Sulaymān's reign.' Or 'they followed the lies the devils uttered against Sulaymān's reign.'

[42] Ṣadūq, Shaykh Muḥammad b. 'Alī, *'Ilal al-Sharāi'*, Vol. 1, p. 20.

Shaykh Muḥammad b. ʿAlī Ṣadūq ﵀ reported[43] another long narration that mentioned the meeting between Saʿd b. ʿAbdullāh al-Ashʿarī ﵀ and Imām Ḥasan al-ʿAskarī ﵇ and his son al-Ḥujjah [Imām Muḥammad al-Mahdī] ﵇. Many responded and commented on this narration until al-Najashī ﵀ said:

> "He had met our Master Abū Muḥammad ﵇, and some of our companions discredit his meeting with Abū Muḥammad ﵇, saying that this story was [wrongly] attributed to him."[44]

Furthermore, Āyatullāh Sayyid Abū al-Qāsim Mūsawī Khū'ī ﵀ commented on a narration as follows:

> "Al-Ṣadūq reported the story of Saʿd's meeting with Abū Muḥammad ﵇ in *Kamāl al-Dīn*, the chapter on reports of who witnessed, saw, and talked to al-Qā'im عجل الله تعالى فرجه الشريف:
>
> > It is narrated that Muḥammad b. ʿAlī b. Muḥammad b. Ḥātim al-Nawfalī, known as al-Karmānī, said: Abū al-ʿAbbās Aḥmad b. ʿĪsā al-Washā' al-Baghdādī narrated to us: Aḥmad b. Ṭāhir al-Qummī narrated to us: Muḥammad b. Bahr b. Sahl al-Shaybānī narrated to us...'. The chain of

43 Ṣadūq, Shaykh Muḥammad b. ʿAlī, *Kamāl al-Dīn wa Tamām al-Niʿma*, p. 454.

44 al-Najāshī, Aḥmad, *al-Fihrist*, p. 177.

> narrators of this narration is fragile, and that is because Muḥammad b. Bahr b. Sahl al-Shaybānī is not trustworthy, and he was accused of exaggeration [ghulūw], in addition to other unknown men in the chain of narrators and the fact that it involves two matters that cannot be believed."[45]

None of his narrations are valid, except for the account of Imām Ja'far al-Ṣādiq's ﷺ lamentation for his son al-Mahdī ﷺ, which was reported by Shaykh Muḥammad b. 'Alī Ṣadūq ﷺ[46] and Shaykh Muḥammad b. Ḥasan Ṭūsī ﷺ.[47]

Ultimately, we conclude that the man was accused of exaggeration [ghulūw] in the Shī'a community and was inaccurate in his reports. Instead, he narrated any and everything, and he would follow the strangest of reports, as was mentioned previously. This demonstrates that his books were widespread among the Ghulāt; hence, it is likely that they also manipulated and distorted the contents of these books.

Therefore, all those above indicate that the chain of narrators of this account is defective and brimming with issues in its entirety. Commenting on the same chain of

---

[45] Khū'ī, Āyatullāh Sayyid Abū al-Qāsim Mūsawī, *Mu'jam Rijāl al-Ḥadīth*, Vol. 9, p. 82.

[46] Ṣadūq, Shaykh Muḥammad b. 'Alī, *Kamāl al-Dīn wa Tamām al-Ni'ma*, p. 352.

[47] Ṭūsī, Shaykh Muḥammad b. Ḥasan, *al-Ghaybah*, p. 167.

narrators in another narration, Āyatullāh Sayyid Abū al-Qāsim Mūsawī Khū'ī 🕮 reinforces our conclusion, saying the following:

"The chain of narrators of this narration is fragile, for Muḥammad b. Bahr b. Sahl al-Shaybānī is not trustworthy and is accused of exaggeration [ghulūw], in addition to the presence of other unknown men in the chain of narrators."[48]

## Examining the Content of the Narration [Matn]

The issues with this narration do not end with its chain of narrators; instead, the content is problematic as well, for it includes some matters that weaken the account and its reliability:

First: In this account, Narjis 🕮 introduced herself as "Malīka, the daughter of Yashua, son of the Caesar of the Romans", meaning that she, aged 13 years old, was the granddaughter of the king of the Romans at that time. As such, by examining these links, we can identify the real identity of her grandfather, the emperor of the Romans. According to this narration, these events occurred during the lifetime of Imām 'Alī al-Hādī 🕮—i.e., before the year 254 AH. Converting this date from Hijri to Georgian format, we would find that these events happened before

---

[48] Khū'ī, Āyatullāh Sayyid Abū al-Qāsim Mūsawī, *Mu'jam Rijāl al-Ḥadīth*, Vol. 9, p. 82.

the year 868 A.C. Tracing the history of the Byzantine dynasty and the names of its emperors, we find that the person referred to in this narration is Michael III who ruled from 842 to 867 A.C. However, this contradicts the narration as this emperor's father, Theophilus, died in 842 A.C. when Michael was still young and not eligible to rule. So, his mother took over the country's reins on his behalf. In this regard, Ibn Kathīr said:

> "The king of the Romans, Theophilos, son of Michael, died in 227 AH after ruling for 12 years. His wife Theodora ruled the Romans after him, and her son Michael, son of Theophilos, was still young."[49]

It is not plausible that someone too young to rule in the year 227 AH would become a grandfather and have a 13-year-old granddaughter less than 25 years later!

Another issue is that the narration mentions the king's desire to marry his daughter (Malīka) to one of his nephews ("My grandfather, the Caesar, wanted to marry me to his nephew"). However, King Theophilos did not have other sons besides Michael, who was very young at that time! Furthermore, if he were to have younger sons, we would circle back to the initial issue: the possibility of this alleged brother having sons of the age of marriage.

---

[49] Ibn Kathīr, *al-Bidāyah wa-l-Nihāyah*, Vol. 10, p. 326.

Hence, we conclude that no Roman emperor fits the description outlined in the narration at that time.

Some[50] suggested that the narration refers not to the Roman emperor but to his high-ranking minister and the actual manager of governmental affairs, Bardas, who achieved the title of Caesar according to history books.[51] However, this possibility is negated as the narration explicitly mentions the word "king" when introducing Narjis ﷺ as "Malīka, the daughter of Yashua, the son of Caesar, *King* of the Romans." Thus, Bardas cannot be the Caesar mentioned in the narration because he was never a king; instead, he was under the emperorship of Michael III. Instead, this possibility suggests that the narrator could not distinguish between the titles of king and Caesar, thus imagining that Bardas was the king of the Romans.

Second, Let us assume that such an emperor (as described in the narration) exists. One issue remains: the narration mentioned a war between the Muslims and the Romans:

> ("...Abū Muḥammad ﷺ told me that my grandfather will shortly be dispatching an army to fight the

[50] al-Ḥasanī, ʿAbd al-Hādī, *al-Sayyidah Narjis ﷺ Salīlah al-Imbrāṭūriyyah al-Bizanṭiyyah wa-Wālidah Munqidh al-Bashariyyah*

[51] Durant, Will and Ariel, *The Story of Civilization, (Qiṣṣat al-Ḥaḍārah)*, Vol. 14, p. 163.

> Muslims on such and such day and that he will follow them...").

However, referring to history books, we cannot find such battles between both sides in that period. Instead, history reports that a ransom deal was made for prisoners between the Muslims and the Romans at that time. Gregory Bar Hebraeus said:

> "In the year 231, the ransom deal between the Muslims and the Romans was made at the hands of Khaqān, the servant of al-Rashīd, and the Muslims gathered on the Lemos river, a day away from Tarsus by foot. Al-Wāthiq Khāqān, the servant of al-Rashīd, ordered that the Muslim prisoners be tested; whoever says that the Qur'ān is created and that God cannot be seen in the Hereafter is ransomed and given a dinar, and whoever does not declare this is left in the custody of the Romans. On the day of 'Āshūrā', the Romans came with the prisoners, and they exchanged prisoners with the Muslims; the Muslims would release a [Roman] prisoner, and the Romans would release a [Muslim] prisoner at the time, and both would meet in the middle of the bridge. When a prisoner would reach the Muslims, they would do takbīr, and when the Romans would receive a prisoner, they would yell "Karialison". The number of Muslim prisoners was 4460, 800

> women and children, and 100 Dhimmis [non-Muslims living in an Islamic state with legal protection]."[52]

This account indicates that the era of Michael III was one of peace and truce between both sides and that the devastating wars mentioned in the narrations happened in the time of his father, Theophilos, son of Michael, and the recurrence of battles happened in the era of whoever came after Michael III. As for the period from the year 250 to 254, during which a war allegedly [as per the narration] took place, we did not find any historical account that proves the occurrence of such a conflict between the Romans and the Muslims, and I do not think that historians would overlook reporting such a war, as all necessities and means for transmission were present at that time.

Some others[53] suggested that the war being referred to is the one that occurred in 249 AH between the Muslims and the Romans, of which Ibn Kathīr documented some events. In this regard, he says:

> "In the year 249, on a Friday in the middle of Rajab, a group of Muslims met a group of Romans near Malatya, and they engaged in a severe battle, resulting in many casualties on both sides. The prince of

[52] Ibn al-ʿIbrī, Grigorios b. Hārūn al-Malāṭī, *Tārīkh Mukhtaṣar al-Duwal*, p. 142.

[53] Marhūn, Shaykh Ḥusayn, *al-Amīrah al-Muqaddasah*.

> Muslims 'Umar b. 'Ubaydullāh b. al-Aqṭā was killed along with one thousand Muslim men, as well as 'Alī b. Yaḥyā al-Armani was also a prince in a sect of Muslims. Indeed, we belong to God, and Him we return. These two princes were great advocates of Islam."[54]

However, once again, this possibility is also negated, owing to the details of this battle that al-Ṭabarī reported in *Tārīkh al-Ṭabarī*, where he said,

> "In the conquest of Ja'far b. Dīnār, called al-Sā'ifah, established a fortress and landfills, and 'Umar b. 'Ubaydullāh al-Aqṭā took his permission to go towards the lands of the Romans with many others of the people of Malatya. The king met him with a great force of Romans in the Bishops Meadow. They fought a great battle, resulting in many casualties from both sides, until the Romans surrounded 'Umar with a hulking force of 50,000 warriors. 'Umar and a thousand Muslim men were then killed on a Friday in the middle of Rajab."[55]

What is important to consider from this extract is that the Romans defeated the Muslims after surrounding them from every side, even killing their leaders. As is typical in wars, the victorious side is the one to capture the remaining from the defeated side as captives, and not vice versa! So,

---

[54] Ibn Kathīr, *al-Bidāyah wa-l-Nihāyah*, Vol. 11, p. 6.

[55] Muḥammad al-Ṭabarī, *Tārīkh al-Ṭabarī*, Vol. 9, p. 261.

this raises the question: How was this Roman woman captured when her country's army emerged victorious over the Muslim armies that were vanquished, as evidenced in the two texts above?

Third: The narration mentions that she is Roman and that Imām ʿAlī al-Hādī ﷺ bought her for his son Imām Ḥasan al-ʿAskarī ﷺ, informing her that she will be the mother of Imām Muḥammad al-Mahdī. However, these details wildly contradict many of the other bodies of narrations from various sources:

- One body of narration indicates that she is Nubian.
- Another indicates that she was born in the ʿAlawī household.
- Another indicates that she belonged to Ḥakīmah ﷺ.
- Another indicates that Ḥakīmah gave her to Imām Ḥasan al-ʿAskarī ﷺ

So, is it logical to reject all these narrations from various sources, many chains, and different narrators for the sake of al-Raḥnī's narration despite its significant weakness?

We shall suffice with these three points despite other issues in the narration; however, for brevity, we have refrained from delving into them so that the book only turns into a discussion of this narration.

## Final Verdict of the Narration

Based on all those above, the account about the mother of Imām Muḥammad al-Mahdī being from the Roman lands suffers from several issues in its chain of narrators [sanad] and content [matn], thus preventing it from being authentic and reliable. Instead, I am almost sure that the story is a figment of imagination propagated by the Ghulāt [those who exaggerate in belief] at that time. There is much resemblance between this narration and the Persian literature (e.g., stories and legends) that was written around the story of Shīrīn and Farhād, thus implying that the person who came up with this narration belonged to a Persian environment, and this matches what we have previously reported about the environment that al-Raḥnī lived in and how his books were widespread in Khurāsān.

Indeed, reading some parts of this report removes any doubt in this matter:

> "There must be a buyer that soothes my heart" / "You have abandoned me, my beloved, while your love fully occupied my heart" / "How could I not when he has been visiting me every night...".

These expressions greatly resemble the romantic stories that are widespread in Persian literature.[56]

Astonishingly, the story of how Lady Shahzānān, the daughter of Yazdigird, reached Imām al-Ḥusayn ﵇ is remarkably similar to this narration. ʿAllamah Muḥammad Bāqir Majlisī ﵀ reported this story in *Biḥār al-Anwār* as follows:

> "And it is reported that she died after being blessed with him, and rather she had chosen [Imām] al-Ḥusayn ﵇ because she had seen Lady Fāṭimah ﵆ and had reverted to Islam before the Muslim soldiers seized her. Moreover, there is a story that she said: In a dream while I was sleeping before the arrival of Muslim soldiers, I saw as if Muḥammad the Messenger of God ﷺ entered our house with [Imām] al-Ḥusayn ﵇ and proposed to me for him and married me to him. When I woke up in the morning, my heart was swayed by this dream, and it completely occupied my mind. During the following night, I saw Lady Fāṭimah ﵆, the daughter of Muḥammad ﷺ; she came to me and introduced me to Islam, and I thus reverted to Islam.

---

[56] Al-Raḥnī's interest in literature is evident in what is reported about him. Ibn Ḥajar mentioned in *Lisān al-Mizān*, Vol. 5, p. 89, that "he was adept in literature and language." This matches the literary tone of the narration, which was filled with refined literary and poetic devices that can only be the product of a seasoned writer. As such, this reinforces the thought that this report is merely a story authored by this writer.

So she 🕊 said:

> "The overcoming shall happen for the Muslims, and
> soon you will reach my son [Imām] al-Ḥusayn
> safely. No one will afflict you with evil. Lady
> Shahzānān continued: As it happened, I was
> brought to al-Madīnah safely; no one harmed
> me!"[57]

## Deconstructing the Illusion

Some might object, saying that Shaykh Muḥammad b. ʿAlī
Ṣadūq 🕊 reported it in his book and relied on it, so how
can one judge it as a figment of imagination produced by
its author or the Ghulāt? The answer lies in the following:

First, there is no proof that Shaykh Muḥammad b. ʿAlī
Ṣadūq investigated its authenticity in his book *Kamāl al-
Dīn wa Tamām al-Niʿma* or that he relied specifically on
well-established reports only. Furthermore, others
suggested that his reliance on this report is conveyed from
the chapter's name (accounts narrated about Narjis, the
mother of al-Qāʾim 🕊, and her name is Malīka, the
daughter of Yashua, the son of Caesar the King), but this is
not correct as there is a possibility that the chapter was
titled as such by scribes, which is known and familiar
among the people in this field.

---

[57] Majlisī, ʿAllamah Muḥammad Bāqir, *Biḥār al-Anwār*, Vol. 46, p. 11.

Second: As previously mentioned, Shaykh Muḥammad b. ʿAlī Ṣadūq ﷺ criticized the narrations of this man, describing him as one of the Ḥashwiyyah [a deviant sect of anthropomorphists], where he said in *ʿIlal al-Sharāiʿ* the following:

> "The compiler of this book said: I wanted this story to be in this book, and regarding Iblīs, I say that he was not that he was one of the angels, but instead he was one of the jinns, except that he worshiped God among the angels, and Hārūt and Mārūt are two angels, and my saying about them is not what the people of the Ḥashw [a deviant sect of anthropomorphists] say; instead, I believe they were infallible. The verse:

﴿وَاتَّبَعوا ما تَتلو الشَّياطينُ عَلىٰ مُلكِ سُلَيمانَ﴾

﴾*wa-ttabaʿū mā tatlū sh-shayāṭīnu ʿalā mulki sulaymāna wa-mā kafara sulaymānu*﴿

﴾*And they followed what the devils pursued during Sulaymān's reign**﴿[58]

---

[58] Sūrat al-Baqarah, Verse 102.

* Or 'they followed what the devils recited during Sulaymān's reign.'

* Or 'they followed the lies the devils uttered against Sulaymān's reign.'

> means that they followed what the devils recited to King Sulaymān and to what was revealed to the two angels in Babylon, Hārūt and Mārūt, and I ascertained a supporting report about that in the book *'Uyūn Akhbār al-Riḍā* ﷺ.'"[59]

So how can he rely on him?

Third: More importantly, Shaykh Muḥammad b. 'Alī Ṣadūq ؒ reported narrations about the Holy Lady ﷺ that contradict each other, and it is not plausible that he believes all of them to be authentic at the same time.

al-Raḥnī's account indicates that Imām Ḥasan al-'Askarī ﷺ knew of Narjis ﷺ from the very beginning, and his father Imām 'Alī al-Hādī ﷺ bought her for him for this purpose. On the other hand, a few pages later, another narration is reported that mentions a different story:

In *Kamāl al-Dīn*, Shaykh Muḥammad b. 'Alī Ṣadūq narrated with his chain of narrators on the authority of Ḥakīmah ﷺ:

> "She [Lady Narjis] was a bondmaid of mine called Narjis. My nephew [Imām Ḥasan al-'Askarī ﷺ] once visited me, and he gazed at her intently, so I said to him:
>
> > My master if you desire her, shall I send her to you?

---

[59] Ṣadūq, Shaykh Muḥammad b. 'Alī, *'Ilal al-Sharāi'*, Vol. 1, p. 20.

He replied:

> No, aunt. However, I am amazed by her.

I asked:

> What about her amazes you?

He عليه السلام said:

> She will bear a child most precious to God عز وجل and through whom God will fill the Earth with peace and justice just as it had been rampant with corruption and oppression.

So I said:

> Shall I send her to you, my master?

He said:

> Get permission from my father عليه السلام about that.

She [Ḥakīmah] said:

> I got dressed and came to the house of Abū al-Ḥasan [Imām ʿAlī al-Hādī] عليه السلام. I greeted him and sat down.

He told me:

> O blessed one, God, the Blessed, the Exalted, has willed you to partake in the reward and goodness.

Ḥakīmah said:

> So I hurried home and adorned her [Narjis], and I gave her to Abū Muḥammad ﷺ."[60]

This narration is evident in that the bondmaid belonged to Ḥakīmah and not Imām ʿAlī al-Hādī ﷺ, and a proof of that is her saying,

> "She was a bondmaid of mine called Narjis."

Her saying,

> "...and I gave her to Abū Muḥammad ﷺ, is even clearer."

This not only contradicts the narration by Muḥammad b. Bahr al-Raḥnī but also negates it completely. If al-Ṣadūq ﵀ believed in the authenticity of the former account [by al-Raḥnī], he would not have reported such a narration that falsifies it, or he would have commented in a way that removes the contradiction between both reports.

---

[60] Ṣadūq, Shaykh Muḥammad b. ʿAlī, *Kamāl al-Dīn wa Tamām al-Niʿma*, p. 426.

# Her Origin

The investigation into the origin of this Holy Lady ﷺ is a matter that requires a prolonged and close examination, as the reports differ, thus claiming her to be from four different regions:

- Roman
- Sindhi
- Moroccan
- Nubian

We shall discuss these claims of her origins successively in this chapter.

## The Claim that She ﷺ is Roman

In the preceding chapter, it became clear that the lengthy account of how the Holy Lady ﷺ reached the Household of infallibility and purity is false. This raises another equally important question: Was the mother of the Imām ﷺ Roman or not?

With the account of Ibn Bahr being proven false, the most famous proof of her being Roman has also lost its validity. However, some other indicators identify her as Roman and are considered proofs of the authenticity of the narrations above, and they are as follows:

First indicator. Al-Faḍl b. Shādhān ﵁ narrated the following in his book *Ithbāt al-Raj'a*:

"Muḥammad b. 'Abd al-Jabbar narrated to us:

I said to my master [Imām] al-Ḥasan b. 'Alī:

O son of the Messenger of God—may God sacrifice me for you—I would love to know who the Imām and God's Ḥujjah [proof of God to humanity] over His servants is after you.

He ﵇ said:

The Imām and Ḥujjah after me is my son; he was named after the Messenger of God ﷺ, and his title is also similar: the seal of the Hujjaj [plural of Ḥujjah] of God and the last of his Vicegerents.

I asked:

Who is his mother, O son of the Messenger of God?

He said:

His mother is the daughter of the son of Caesar, king of the Romans, but when he is born, he will be concealed from the people for a long occultation, after which he shall emerge and kill

> the Dajjāl, filling the Earth with peace and justice just as it was rampant with corruption and oppression; so it is not permissible for anyone to call him with his name or his title before his emergence, God's blessings upon him."[61]

This narration indicates that the mother of Imām Muḥammad al-Mahdī is the daughter of the son of Caesar, king of the Romans, so there is no comment on this. However, there are points to discuss regarding the source of this narration that prevent us from relying on it:

First, We did not receive the book *Ithbāt al-Raj'a* by al-Fadl b. Shādhān al-Nīshābūrī among the books that reached us; instead, we received some of his narrations scattered across some works of the companions. The narration above was reported by al-Ḥurr al-'Āmilī ﷺ in *Ithbāt al-Hudāt*[62] and al-Mīrlūḥī al-Iṣfahānī ﷺ in *Kifāyat al-Muhtadī*[63]. In this regard, there is much to talk about the copy of the book that reached both of them; an experienced person would notice how this book was not well-known before the eleventh century, as almost no one quoted anything from the book. In addition to that, al-Ḥurr al-'Āmilī ﷺ stated

---

61 *Majallat Turāthunā*, Vol. 15, p. 212.

62 al-Ḥurr al-'Āmilī, Shaykh Muḥammad, *Ithbāt al-Hudāt bil-Nuṣūṣ wal-Mu'jizāt*, Vol. 5, p. 196.

63 *Mukhtasar Kifāyat al-Muhtadī*, p. 108.

that the copy he received was "bajada," meaning that it was found handwritten by someone else; in this regard, he said:

> "This is what we found reported from al-Fadl b. Shādhān's work of *Ithbāt al-Raj'a* in the handwriting of some distinguished scholars of ḥadīth [Muhaddithīn]."[64]

The same is the case for al-Mīrlūḥī, as we know nothing about the copy that reached him except for what he mentioned about obtaining a copy of the book *al-Ghaybah* without clarifying how he got it or providing any beneficial details. Therefore, the first issue we face is the need for more trust in the authenticity of the copy from which this account was reported.

Second, what further deepens the mistrust in this copy is that it does not match the narrations of al-Fadl b. Shādhān ﷺ is present in other books. This raises a question: If this is the [correct] copy of the book known to the first-comers, then why do we not find these narrations in their books even though they reported many accounts on the authority of al-Fadl b. Shādhān ﷺ?

Strange indeed, the narrations in this book copy are impeccable, and its chains of transmission are correct and highly considered. So, is it plausible that the most outstanding scholars of ḥadīth [Muḥaddithīn] of the sect

---

[64] The manuscript of *Ithbāt al-Raj'a*, which is found in *al-Maktabah al-Ridhawiyah* [the Imām Ridha Library in Mashhad, Irān.]

would overlook it and instead report from books of lower authenticity and lesser-known chains of transmission?

Third: The final point is that this narration, which is used to identify the mother of Imām Muḥammad al-Mahdī, is narrated by Muḥammad b. 'Abd al-Jabbār. However, I searched through many books of ḥadīth, al-Rijāl, and biographies, but I could not find any narration by al-Fadl on the authority of a "Muḥammad b. 'Abd al-Jabbār". This discrepancy further deepens our doubt about the authenticity of the copy at hand!

Therefore, it is impossible to rely on this narration due to the above-mentioned factors.

Second indicator. Another point that is used to identify her as Roman is what is reported in the following Ziyārat of the Holy Lady Narjis عليها السلام:

> "Peace be upon the mother of the Imām and the lady entrusted with the secrets of the Knowing King, and the bearer of the most honorable of all beings.
>
> Peace be upon you, O veracious and well-pleased lady.
>
> Peace be upon you, O equivalent of [Prophet] Mūsā's mother and daughter of [Prophet] 'Īsā's Disciple.
>
> Peace be upon you, O pious, and bring one.

> Peace be upon you, O well-pleased and well-contented one.
>
> Peace be upon you, O you, the one described in the Gospel, the one betrothed from the Honest Spirit of God, the one with whom Muḥammad, the chief of the Messengers, wished to connect, the one entrusted with the secrets of the Lord of the Worlds.
>
> Peace be upon you and your fathers, the Disciples.
>
> Peace be upon you, your husband, and your son. Peace be upon you and your pure spirit and body."[65]

Al-Mashhadī saved us from prolonging the discussion on this Ziyārat, as he mentioned in its introduction:

> "The Ziyārat of the mother of al-Qā'im was dictated to me by a man from Bahrain whom I had heard reciting it."[66]

This highlights that the Ziyārat is not transmitted from the infallible ones; instead, it is the work of an unknown man whom Shaykh al-Mashhadī said to be from Bahrain. Perhaps he penned this Ziyārat based on the famous narration, which is the case for the Ziyārat that are made

---

[65] al-Mashhadī, Muḥammad, *al-Mazār al-Kabīr*,, p. 660.

[66] Ibid.

for some of the offspring of the infallible ﷺ based on narrations reported about them.

As such, it becomes apparent that there is no solid proof that Imām Muḥammad al-Mahdī's mother was Roman. The proposed indicators do not serve as valid proof for this claim that has become famous and has spread like wildfire with no valid basis or foundation.

## The Claim that She ﷺ is Sindhi

Some attempted to establish that the mother of Imām Muḥammad al-Mahdī comes from Sindh. This claim is propagated based on what al-Ḥusayn b. Ḥamdān al-Khaṣībī reported from his chains of transmission on the authority of Ḥakīmah, daughter of Imām Muḥammad al-Jawād ﷺ, narrating that she came to Abū Muḥammad [Imām Ḥasan al-ʿAskarī] ﷺ and prayed for God to bestow upon him a son and that she said:

> I came to him and told him and prayed for him as I always do.
>
> So he said:
>
>> O aunt, the son you are praying to God to bless me with will be born on this night—it was a Friday night after eight nights had passed from the month of Shaʿbān, in the year 257 AH—so break your fast with us.

She said:

> O my master, who bears this great son?

He said:

> Narjis, O aunt.

She said:

> Indeed, she is my most beloved among your bondmaids.

Ḥakīmah said:

> I got up, and then went to her and did as she [Narjis] usually does, and Narjis spoke to me in Sindhi, so I replied to her in the same, throwing myself at her hands and kissing them.

So Narjis said:

> May God sacrifice me for you. In return, I told her: Rather may God sacrifice me for you and all the worlds.

Narjis rejected that, so I said:

> You deny what I did; how could you be shy in front of me when, indeed, God will bless you on this night with a Master of this world and the

Hereafter, and he shall be the salvation for the believers.[67]

The proof in this narration is her saying,

"I got up, and then went to her and did as she [Narjis] usually does, and Narjis spoke to me in Sindhi..."

This part indicates that she 🌸 spoke Sindhi, which likens the possibility that she came from Sindh.

However, this argument can be refuted with the following points:

First: Shaykh Muḥammad b. ʿAlī Ṣadūq 🌸 and Shaykh Muḥammad b. Ḥasan Ṭūsī 🌸 reported this narration *without* the statement that is used as proof of this claim. As such, this appears to be an insertion solely propagated by al-Khaṣībī and no one else, and it has been established in such a case that insertion is not accepted unless it comes from a source of reliable and trust and is not contradicted otherwise; however, all this is absent in this regard. Al-Khaṣībī was criticized by all those who wrote about him, highlighting his sect's corruption and distortion in his books. It is sufficient for an experienced person [in this field] to compare al-Khaṣībī's narrations and the ones reported by those of great trustworthiness and reliability to note the significant difference.

---

67 Khaṣībī, Ḥusayn b. Ḥamadān, *al-Hidāyat al-Kubrā*, p.355.

Second, some who investigated this part specifically concluded that it was missing from all book manuscripts. By reviewing some of the manuscripts available at hand, it becomes apparent that the word "Sindhi" came from the word "Siyada" [lordship, title of respect], and this is actually in line with the context of the conversation and what the narration reported by Shaykh Muḥammad b. ʿAlī Ṣadūq and al-Ṭūsī indicate as follows:

> "When I greeted her and sat down, she came to take off my slippers and said to me:
>
> > O my mistress and the mistress of my family, how are you?
>
> So I said to her:
>
> > Rather, you are my mistress and the mistress of my family.
>
> She rejected this and said:
>
> > What is this that you are saying, O aunt?
>
> I said:
>
> > O, daughter, God The Almighty will bestow upon you in your night a son who is a master in this world and the Hereafter.

At that, she became humble and shy."[68]

What is meant by "she spoke to me with 'Siyada'" is that she [Narjis] addressed Lady Ḥakīmah ﷺ with the title "my mistress" [Sayyidatī], so she replied to her with the same, saying, "Rather you are my mistress and the mistress of my family," as evident in the narration. It is sufficient to only look at al-Khaṣībī's account to infer that the context indicates this meaning instead, not what he reported about talking in Sindhi.

Third: If we were to assume that the word "Sindhi" is present, then there remains an issue: one does not need to be of Sindhi origin to know its tongue and speak the Sindhi language. Perhaps the person learned the language from somewhere. The report indicated that Ḥakīmah, daughter of Imām Muḥammad al-Jawād ﷺ, spoke Sindhi as well, so does this necessitate that she is of Sindhi origin?

Thus, this narration cannot be relied upon regarding the presence of the word "Sindhi" nor its implications. Therefore, there is no proof that she ﷺ is Sindhi.

---

[68] Ṣadūq, Shaykh Muḥammad b. ʿAlī, *Kamāl al-Dīn wa Tamām al-Niʿma*, p. 424.

## The Claim that She ﷺ is Moroccan

Some contemporary scholars,[69] may God protect them, mentioned the possibility that Lady Narjis ﷺ came from Morocco. In this sense, Shaykh ʿAlī al-Kūrānī al-ʿĀmilī said: "It seems that the word "Black" in the copy of al-Nuʿmānī has been inserted, as the narrations agree that the mother of Imām Muḥammad al-Mahdī is Roman or Moroccan, and not Black."[70]

However, I searched the private books for a narration that implies this, but to no avail. Then I went through the public books for the same purpose, yet I could not find anything that reinforces what the Shaykh, may God protect him, said.[71] The closest information I came upon in this regard were some reports that state that Imām Muḥammad al-Mahdī ﷺ will emerge from the lands of Morocco. This was reported by al-Qurṭubī, where he says:

> "The ḥadīth of Umm Salama and Abū Hurayrah indicates that people will pledge allegiance to al-Mahdī between the Rukn [Corner] and the maqām [of the Kaʿbah], but it appears not to be as such since Ibn Masʿūd and other Ṣaḥābah narrated that he will emerge

---

[69] Shaykh ʿAlī al-Kūrāni al-ʿĀmilī, may God maintain his merits.

[70] *Muʿjam Aḥadīth al-Imām Muḥammad al-Mahdī* ﷺ, Vol. 3, p. 239.

[71] I tried many times to contact Shaykh ʿAlī al-Kūrāni al-ʿĀmilī, may God protect him, but to no avail, especially after his latest illness.

> at the end of time from Morocco, and he will walk 40 miles with victory on his hands, and his banners are white and yellow inscribed with the Great Name of God. None of his banners will be defeated. These banners will emerge from the sea coast at Masnah in Morocco."[72]

Even if we accept these narrations, his ﷺ emergence from Morocco does not mean that his mother is Moroccan.

## The Claim that She ﷺ is Nubian

Finally, the claim that she ﷺ is of Nubian origin is based on several groups of narrations, some of which are direct proofs of this claim, and others are supporting elements:

The first proof is what Shaykh Muḥammad b. Yaʿqūb Kulaynī narrated in *al-Kāfī*:

"On the authority of ʿAlī b. Ibrāhīm, his father, and ʿAlī b. Muḥammad al-Qāsanī, on the authority of Zakariyyā b. Yaḥyā b. al-Nuʿmān al-Sayrafī...

> ʿAlī b. Jaʿfar said:
>
> > I got up and kissed Abū Jaʿfar ﷺ, and then I said to him:

---

[72] al-Qurṭubī, Shams al-Dīn Muḥammad b. Aḥmad, *Tadhkirah bi Aḥwāl al-Mawtā wa Umūr al-Ākhirah*, p. 1206.

> I bear witness in front of God that you are my Imām.

So al-Riḍā ﷺ wept and said:

> O uncle, did you not hear my father when he said, 'The Messenger of God ﷺ:

May my father be sacrificed for the son of the best of the bondmaids, the son of the sweet-mouthed Nubian lady who was chosen to give birth to this purified son. May the curse of God be upon the ʿUbaydīs [the ʿAbbāsids] and their descendants, the instigators of strife [fitnah], and may they suffer greatly and be subject to torture, humiliation, and death for years, months, and days [at the hand of al-Qā'im ﷺ when he reappears or by God]. He is the one in occultation, the one who was persecuted and left without a home, the one who could not avenge the blood of his father and his grandfather. People wonder: did he die or perish? What path did he walk?'

> O uncle, he is surely from me [my descendant].

So I said:

> You are truthful; may I be sacrificed for you."[73]

[73] Kulaynī, Shaykh Muḥammad b. Yaʿqūb, *al-Kāfī*, Vol. 1, p. 322.

The proof is in his saying,

> "May my father be sacrificed for the son of the best of the bondmaids, the son of the sweet-mouthed Nubian..."

The conversation here is not about Imām Muḥammad al-Jawād ﷺ but about Imām Muḥammad al-Mahdī ﷺ, as is evident from his saying,

> "He is the owner of the Occultation, the one who was persecuted and left without a home, the home could not avenge the blood of his father and his grandfather."

These attributes are specific to the Seal of the Vicegerents and cannot be given to others. Similarly, the expression "the best of the bondmaids" was also reported in other narrations about the mother of Imām Muḥammad al-Mahdī, and not about anyone else. It is narrated that Amīr al-Mu'minīn ﷺ said:

> May my father be sacrificed for the son of the best of bondmaids—referring to al-Qā'im ﷺ from his progeny ﷺ—they shall taste the worst of pain and suffering.[74]

Based on this, al-Māzandarānī ﷺ concluded that the Nubian mother mentioned therein is the mother of the

---

[74] Ṭūsī, Shaykh Muḥammad b. Ḥasan, *al-Ghaybah*, p. 234.

Imām of the Time ﷹ; commenting on this narration, he said:

> "His saying (the son of the best of bondmaids) refers to the Imām of the Time ﷹ and not Imām Muḥammad al-Jawād ﷷ because the pronoun in 'he was the one who was persecuted' certainly refers to the Imām of the Time, describing his situation. Moreover, regarding the saying 'son of the Nubian', Nubia is a spacious region in Sudan next to Upper Egypt, including Abyssinia, and Nubia is also a mountain in Sudan. The people from this region are called Nubian."[75]

On the other hand, ʿAllamah Muḥammad Bāqir Majlisī ﵀ determined that, indeed, it is Imām Muḥammad al-Mahdī ﷹ who is being referred to, but attributing him to the Nubian mother is a figurative expression, as the Nubian mother is the mother of Imām Muḥammad al-Jawād ﷷ, and as such, she is also considered to be the mother of Imām Muḥammad al-Mahdī via [the bond of] progeny. In this regard, he said:

> "The expression 'the son of the best...' refers to Imām Muḥammad al-Mahdī ﷹ; as for the expression '...the best of the bondmaids' refers to the mother of Imām Muḥammad al-Jawād ﷷ, for she is considered his [Imām Muḥammad al-Mahdī] mother via [the bond

[75] al-Māzandarānī, al-Mawlā Muḥammad Ṣāliḥ b. Aḥmad, *Sharḥ Uṣūl al-Kāfī*, Vol. 6, p. 212.

of] progeny. As for his actual immediate mother, she is the daughter of Caesar, and she was not Nubian."[76]

His words ﷺ contradict the apparent meaning of the text, for attributing her motherhood to the Imām via the bond of progeny is a type of metaphor that lacks a presumption for it to be possible to stray away from the apparent meaning. Suppose it is said that ʿAllamah Muḥammad Bāqir Majlisī ﷺ did indeed mention a presumption, which is what indicates that the mother of Imām Muḥammad al-Mahdī is Roman. In that case, we counter that we have thoroughly discussed this matter such that it cannot be used as a presumption to stray away from the apparent meaning of the text.

On the other hand, an issue might arise with the argument of her Nubian origin and the proof in the narration above: Shaykh Muḥammad b. Muḥammad b. Nuʿmān Mufīd ﷺ narrated this report in the book *al-Irshād* but with a different wording that changed the meaning entirely. He reported the following:

"Abū al-Qāsim Jaʿfar b. Muḥammad told me on the authority of Muḥammad b. Yaʿqūb, on the authority of ʿAlī b. Ibrāhīm b. Hāshim, on the authority of his father and ʿAlī b. Muḥammad al-Qāsanī, all together on the authority of Zakariyyā b. Yaḥyā b. al-Nuʿmān:

---

[76] Majlisī, ʿAllamah Muḥammad Bāqir, *Mir'āt al-ʿUqūl fī Sharḥ Akhbār Āl al-Rasūl*, Vol. 3, p. 381.

I heard ʿAlī b. Jaʿfar b. Muḥammad speaking to al-Ḥasan b. al-Ḥusayn b. ʿAlī b. al-Ḥusayn, during which he said:

> God helped Abū al-Ḥasan [Imām ʿAlī] al-Riḍā when his brothers and uncles oppressed him.

He then mentioned a long ḥadīth, at the end of which he said:

> So I got up and grabbed the hand of Abū Jaʿfar Muḥammad b. ʿAlī al-Riḍā and said to him:
>
>> I bear witness in front of God that you are my Imām.
>
> So al-Riḍā wept and said:
>
>> O uncle, did you not hear my father when he said:
>>
>>> The Messenger of God said:
>>>
>>>> May my father be sacrificed for the son of the best of the bondmaids, the virtuous Nubian; from among his [Imām ʿAlī al-Riḍā] offsprings will come the one who was persecuted and left without a home, the one who could not avenge the blood of his father and his grandfather, the one in occultation.

> People wonder: did he die or perish? What path did he walk?

So I said:

> You are truthful; may I be sacrificed for you."[77]

The report, conversely, indicates that the son of the Nubian mother is Imām Muḥammad al-Jawād ﷷ and that the persecuted one left without a home and the one of the Occultation is his offspring Imām al-Mahdī ﷷ, thus preventing this narration altogether from being a proof for this claim.

However, this report cannot be used to discredit the narration above, and that is because Shaykh Muḥammad b. Muḥammad b. Nuʿmān Mufīd ﷷ stated that he transmitted this narration from the book of *al-Kāfī* by Shaykh Muḥammad b. Yaʿqūb Kulaynī ﷷ, which is evident from the chain of transmission. We found no discrepancy between all copies of al-Kāfī available to us; instead, they all report the above narration. Hence, there seems to be a discrepancy [in al-Mufīd's case] in transmission because Shaykh Muḥammad b. Muḥammad b. Nuʿmān Mufīd ﷷ reported the narration in meaning and not literally word for word, and a proof of this is his saying,

---

[77] Mufīd, Shaykh Muḥammad, *Kitāb al-Irshād*, Vol. 2, p. 275.

"He then mentioned a long ḥadīth, at the end of which he said...".[78]

Regarding the supporting group of narrations, among them is what was reported about Imām Muḥammad al-Mahdī ﷺ being the son of a black bondmaid, and there are many narrations in this regard:

Among these narrations is what al-Nuʿmānī ؒ reported in his book *al-Ghaybah*:

"Aḥmad b. Muḥammad b. Saʿīd b. ʿUqda narrated to us: Muḥammad b. al-Mufaḍḍal b. Qays b. Rumāna al-Ashʿarī, Saʿdan b. Isḥāq b. Saʿīd, Aḥmad b. al-Ḥusayn b. ʿAbd al-Mālik, and Muḥammad b. al-Ḥasan al-Qaṭuānī, all narrated to us: al-Ḥasan b. Mahbūt al-Zarad narrated to us on the authority of Hishām b. Sālim, on the authority of Yazīd al-Kanāsī:

I heard Abū Jaʿfar [Imām Muḥammad] al-Bāqir ﷺ say:

Indeed, Ṣāḥib al-Amr [i.e., one of the titles of Imām Muḥammad al-Mahdī, literally meaning 'lord of the cause'] has a resemblance to Yūsuf; the son of a Black bondmaid, and God resolves his affairs in one night."[79]

---

[78] Ibid.

[79] Ṭūsī, Shaykh Muḥammad b. Ḥasan, *al-Ghaybah*, p. 166.

The report highlights a single truth: the mother of the Imām ﷺ is a black bondmaid, and this is an apparent contradiction to the narration that suggests that she is Roman, for we did not hear of there being dark-skinned people among the Romans. Moreover, this report also provides us with a preliminary conception of this great woman's land; at that time, black slaves were mainly from the African continent, particularly from the lands of Abyssinia and Nubia, i.e., the triangle of Sudan, Ethiopia, and Eritrea.

It is strange that a contemporary scholar[80] denies the presence of the wording "black" in the narration, where he said:

> "It seems that the word 'black' is an insertion in al-Nuʿmānī's copy, as the narrations collectively agree that the mother of Imām Muḥammad al-Mahdī is Roman or Moroccan, and she is not Black."[81]

This statement raises a few counterpoints:

First: All copies of the book *al-Ghaybah* by al-Nuʿmānī report this narration with the same wording (Black bondmaid), and we did not find a single copy where this

---

[80] Shaykh ʿAlī al-Kūrāni al-ʿĀmilī, may God maintain his merits.

[81] *Muʿjam Aḥadīth al-Imām Muḥammad al-Mahdī* ﷺ, Vol. 3, p. 239.

term (Black) was missing. Therefore, the issue above loses ground and becomes merely a guess with no base.

Second: What al-Nuʿmānī ﵀ mentioned at the end of the chapter is indicative of his approval of this group of narrations that clearly state that she ﵏ was a black bondmaid, for he said:

> "O you who see with the light of guidance, whose hearts are free of blindness and are radiating faith and light, consider what the two Imāms [Imām Muḥammad al-Bāqir and Imām Jaʿfar al-Ṣādiq] ﵉ have said about the Occultation [al-Ghaybah], about how a al-Qāʾim ﷼ follows in the prophets' ﵈ paths filled with concealment and fear, that he is the son of a black bondmaid, and that God will resolve his affairs in one night."[82]

This concretely validates the authenticity of the wording (black) in this narration, allowing for no further doubt.

Third: This narration was also reported in another source and with another chain of transmission. In *Kamāl al-Dīn*, Shaykh Muḥammad b. ʿAlī Ṣadūq ﵀ said:

"Abd al-Wāḥid b. Muḥammad b. ʿAbdus ﵀ narrated to us: Abū ʿAmrū al-Kāshī narrated to us: Muḥammad b. Masʿūd narrated to us: ʿAlī b. Muḥammad al-Qummī narrated to

[82] Ṭūsī, Shaykh Muḥammad b. Ḥasan, *al-Ghaybah*, p. 168.

us, on the authority of Muḥammad b. Aḥmad b. Yaḥyā, on the authority of Ibrāhīm b. Hāshim, on the authority of Abū Aḥmad al-Azadī, on the authority of Dhāris al-Kanāsī:

I heard Abū Jaʿfar 🕮 say:

> Indeed, Ṣāḥib al-Amr [i.e., one of the titles of Imām Muḥammad al-Mahdī, literally meaning 'lord of the cause'] has one of the characteristics Yūsuf; the son of a Black bondmaid, and God will resolve his affairs in one night."[83]

Similarly, this report also settles the dispute in this group of narrations, leaving no space for skepticism or doubt in that Imām Muḥammad al-Mahdī 🕮 is the son of a black bondmaid. In turn, this validates the authenticity of the account above that she 🕮 is a [Nubian] woman from the land of Nubia.

Another supporting report is what was narrated about Imām Muḥammad al-Mahdī 🕮 being of dark skin color:

In his book *al-Ghaybah*, Shaykh Muḥammad b. Ḥasan Ṭūsī 🕮 narrated with a chain of transmission on the authority of Jābir al-Jaʿfī on the authority of Abū Jaʿfar 🕮:

---

[83] Ṣadūq, Shaykh Muḥammad b. ʿAlī, *Kamāl al-Dīn wa Tamām al-Niʿma*, p. 329.

> "al-Mahdī is a descendant of Fāṭimah, and he is of 'Adam' skin color [i.e., black or very dark skin color, no whiteness to it]."[84]

Furthermore, Sayyid b. Ṭāwūs narrated with a chain of transmission on the authority of Imām Mūsā al-Kāẓim:

> "May my father be sacrificed for al-Mahdī from the progeny of Muḥammad the one with the wide abdomen, a unibrow, slim legs, broad shoulders, and a dark complexion that is accompanied with a yellowness due to staying up all night.
>
> May my father be sacrificed for him, the one who spends his nights prostrating and bowing [to God].
>
> May my father be sacrificed for the one whom, by God, the blame of a blamer never befalls, the light in the darkness.
>
> May my father be sacrificed for al-Qā'im, the one who upholds the order of God."[85]

Reports describing his physical appearance reinforce that he is of dark skin color. In this regard, Abū al-Adyān narrated:

---

[84] Ṭūsī, Shaykh Muḥammad b. Ḥasan, *al-Ghaybah*, p. 187.

[85] Sayyid 'Alī b. Mūsā b. Ja'far b. Ṭāwūs (Ibn Ṭāwūs), *Falāḥ al-Sā'il wa Najāḥ al-Masā'il* p. 200.

> "When we got to the house, [Imām] al-Ḥasan b. ʿAlī ﷺ was in the coffin, so Jaʿfar b. ʿAlī came forward to pray for his brother. When he started with takbīr, a dark-skinned boy came out, with short curly hair and cleaved teeth, and he grabbed onto the mantle of Jaʿfar b. ʿAlī and said:
>
>> Step aside, O uncle, for I have more right to lead the funeral prayer for my father.
>
> So Jaʿfar stepped aside, his face losing color."[86]

Here, dark skin color does not mean the typical tanned complexion of Arabs; rather, what is meant here is a specific type of dark skin—as mentioned previously—the one called 'Adam', and it is a very dark skin color, as per the dictionaries.

Ultimately, this group of narrations is not an independent proof of this claim. However, it supports those above: it is most logical that one whose mother is Nubian would also be dark-skinned, as opposed to one whose mother is Roman, for his skin color would be closer to white if it were not as such indeed.

The same can be reinforced with the narration from Yaʿqūb al-Dharrāb, which suggests that Imām Muḥammad al-Mahdī ﷺ had an aunt of dark skin color.

---

[86] Ṣadūq, Shaykh Muḥammad b. ʿAlī, *Kamāl al-Dīn wa Tamām al-Niʿma*, p. 475.

In his book *al-Ghaybah*, Shaykh Muḥammad b. Ḥasan Ṭūsī رحمه الله narrated an account with his chain of transmission on the authority of Yaʿqūb b. Yūsuf al-Dharrāb al-Ghasānī, on his departure from Isfahan, said:

> "I performed Ḥajj with a group of people of opposing beliefs [i.e., Sunnīs] from my town in 281 AH. When we reached Makkah, one of our companions rented us a house on Sūq al-Layl Street, and the house was a property of Lady Khadījah عليها السلام, which was known as Dār al-Riḍā عليه السلام. An old lady occupied the house with a dark or wheatish complexion. When I came to know that the house was called Dār al-Riḍā عليه السلام, I asked that old lady how she was related to the owner of the house and why it was called Dār al-Riḍā.
>
> She said,
>
>> I am one of the adherents of the house's owner, and this house belongs to ʿAlī b. Mūsā al-Riḍā عليه السلام. Imām Ḥasan al-ʿAskarī عليه السلام has accommodated me because I had been in his service.
>
> I was delighted upon hearing that, but I did not reveal that information to the [Sunnī] people with me. Whenever I returned from Ṭawāf at night, I slept in the corridor with them. We used to close the door and place a massive stone behind it. One night, I saw a light in the corridor where we slept; it was similar to the light of a lantern. Then the door was opened, but I did not see

anyone from the people of the house opening it. I saw a young man with medium stature and a wheatish complexion; he seemed physically fit and had a prostration mark on his forehead. He wore two shirts, a cloak he cast over his head, and shoes without socks. The man entered and climbed up to the room [or attic] occupied by the old lady. Curiosity overcame me; I wanted to know about this man.

I asked the old lady about him and told her,

> O so-and-so, I want to ask you something in private, but I cannot do it as others are also present. So, when you notice that I am alone in the house, I would like it if you could come down so that I can ask you about something.

She replied hurriedly,

> I also want to speak to you in private, but I have not had the chance because of those accompanying you.

I asked,

> What did you want to tell me?

She said,

> He—[but she did not mention anyone]— has told you not to be harsh with your companions and

> associates and do not dispute with them, for they are your enemies, and it is their house.

I asked,

> Who has said this?

She replied,

> I do.

I felt simultaneous awe and fear, so I dared not ask anything else. I just asked what she meant by companions. I thought she was referring to my present companions with whom I had come for Ḥajj.

But she said,

> Your associates in your town and those with you in the house.

In truth, I had had disputes with my companions in the house with me about religious matters. They began gossiping about me until I ran away from there and went into hiding. Now I understood that she was talking about them.

I asked,

> What is your concern with [Imām] al-Riḍā عليه السلام?

She said,

> I was the servant of [Imām] al-Ḥasan b. ʿAlī ﷺ.

When I became certain that she was connected to that family, I asked her about the Imām in Occultation [al-Ghayb] ﷺ and said,

> I beseech you, tell me if you have seen him yourself!

She said,

> O brother, I have not seen him with my own eyes because when I had left that place, my sister was pregnant, al-Ḥasan b. ʿAlī [Imām Ḥasan al-ʿAskarī] ﷺ had given me the glad tidings that I would see him at the end of my life, and he told me:
>
> > You will be to him as you were to me."[87]

Her saying,

> "O brother, I have not seen him with my own eyes because when I had left that place, my sister was pregnant..."

suggests that this mentioned sister is the mother of Imām Muḥammad al-Mahdī, for how else could a foreign pregnant woman be present in the house of Imām Ḥasan

[87] Ṭūsī, Shaykh Muḥammad b. Ḥasan, *al-Ghaybah*, p. 273.

al-ʿAskarī? And what is the relation between her pregnancy and the question posed by Yaʿqūb al-Dharrāb about the concealed Imām?

Ultimately, these different categories of narrations lead to a reliable conclusion: the mother of our master, Imām Muḥammad al-Mahdī, is a black bondmaid from Nubia.

## The Final Outcome

All that was presented and the discussion of various proofs led to the conclusion that Imām Muḥammad al-Mahdī's mother is likely a bondmaid from Nubia. Furthermore, all that was presented also proves the invalidity of the narration [al-Raḥnī's account claiming her to be of Roman origin] that we had previously mentioned, and it was indeed proven to contradict many narrations about the Ahl al-Bayt.

Therefore, we can now move on from what we mentioned at the beginning of this chapter and thus state that there is proof that the mother of Imām Muḥammad al-Mahdī was not Roman, which was a widespread claim circulating among the people at that time. This research raises another question: how did this pure Nubian woman reach the infallible Holy Household?

# How Did She Reach the Holy Household ﷺ?

With al-Raḥnī's narration above being proven to be invalid, another matter comes forward as a ramification: the mother of Imām Muḥammad al-Mahdī reached the Holy Household after a very long journey of captivity. As such, it is prudent that the discussion now focus on the answer to the question that has become a gap in her biography: how did this holy woman reach the 'Alawī household?

## Did She Belong to Imām 'Alī al-Hādī?

The most important point to start the research on this topic is determining who the owner of the mother of Imām Muḥammad al-Mahdī was, after establishing the fact that she was an owned bondmaid as cited by many narrations. The narration by al-Raḥnī that was discussed previously mentioned that it was Imām Muḥammad al-Mahdī who bought her; however, this contradicts another body of narrations that clearly states that she belonged to Ḥakīmah, the daughter of Imām Muḥammad al-Jawād.

Shaykh Muḥammad b. Ḥasan Ṭūsī reported a long narration about Ḥakīmah, answering someone who had asked her about al-Ḥujjah:

> "O my mistress, did [Imām] al-Ḥasan have a son?

She [Ḥakīmah] smiled and said:

> If [Imām] al-Ḥasan ﷺ did not have a successor, then who is the Ḥujjah [God's sign to mankind] after him? I had told you that the Imāmate does not pass to brothers after [Imām] al-Ḥasan and [Imām] al-Ḥusayn ﷺ.

So I said:

> O my mistress, tell me about the birth of my master and his occultation ﷺ.

She said:

> Yes, she [his mother] was a bondmaid of mine called Narjis. My nephew [Imām Ḥasan al-'Askarī ﷺ] once visited me, and he gazed at her intently, so I said to him:
>
> My master if you desire her, shall I send her to you?

He replied:

> No, aunt. Nevertheless, I am amazed by her.

I asked:

> What about her amazes you?

He 🕊 said:

> She will bear a child most precious to God 🕊 and
> through whom God will fill the earth with peace
> and justice just as it had been rampant with
> corruption and oppression.

So I said:

> Shall I send her to you, my master?

He said:

> Get permission from my father 🕊 about that. So I
> dressed and came to the house of Abū al-Ḥasan
> [Imām ʿAlī al-Hādī] 🕊. I greeted him and sat down.

He started talking before I could and said to me:

> O Ḥakīmah, send Narjis to my son Abū
> Muḥammad [Imām Ḥasan al-ʿAskarī 🕊].

So I said:

> That is why I came here, and I shall take my leave to
> do so.

He told me:

> O blessed one, God, the Blessed, the Exalted, has
> willed you to partake in the reward and goodness.

> So I hurried home and adorned her [Narjis] and gave her to Abū Muḥammad ﷺ, and I united them under my roof, so he stayed at my house for several days before he went to his father ﷺ, and I sent her with him."[88]

Shaykh Muḥammad b. Ḥasan Ṭūsī reported this account as "mursal" [transmitted or sent]:

> "It is narrated that one of the sisters of Abū al-Ḥasan [Imām 'Alī al-Hādī] ﷺ had a bondmaid whom she raised, and she was called Narjis. When she grew up, Abū Muḥammad [Imām Ḥasan al-'Askarī] ﷺ gazed at her once when he entered the room, so she [his sister] said to him:
>
> > I see you, my master, looking at her; why is that?
>
> So he said:
>
> > I only look at her out of amazement as she will bear a newborn most precious to God, The Almighty.
>
> Then he told her to get the permission of Abū al-Ḥasan [Imām 'Alī al-Hādī] ﷺ to send her [Narjis] to him, and she did so."[89]

---

[88] Ṣadūq, Shaykh Muḥammad b. 'Alī, *Kamāl al-Dīn wa Tamām al-Ni'ma*, p. 426.

[89] Ṭūsī, Shaykh Muḥammad b. Ḥasan, *al-Ghaybah*, p. 244.

Two arguments could be raised against this narration involving the following two points:

1. Its mention of Imām Ḥasan al-ʿAskarī 🕮 gazing at Narjis 🕮, for how could such conduct come from the Imām 🕮?

2. It contradicts other authentic narrations that Ḥakīmah 🕮 did not know the identity of al-Qāʾim's mother 🕮.

These issues could be resolved as follows:

As for the first, it is noteworthy that Narjis was a bondmaid and not a free woman, and it is known that it is permissible to gaze at a bondmaid and even touch her and engage in intimacy with her if her owner permitted it. This appears to be the case here, as the context implies the approval of the owner, except that it was not voiced out loud because it is self-evidently clear that such an act would not come from the best people, especially not from a holy figure such as Imām Ḥasan al-ʿAskarī 🕮.

In this regard, Sayyid Muḥammad al-Ṣadr 🕮 gave a great answer when he said:

"The answer is simple and straightforward: he looked at her with the permission of her owner; if the owner permitted someone to look at their bondmaid, then it is permissible to do so within the boundaries of the owner's permission. This was not mentioned in the

> narration; however, it is given in the narration that the Muslim community is well aware that it is not permissible to look[90] at a bondmaid except with the permission of the owner. Therefore, it is evident in the narrator's mind that the Muslim listener will immediately understand that the permission to look was given, thus neglecting to mention it."

As for the second issue, the answer to it is contained inside the narration itself: Ḥakīmah's ﷺ question about the identity of Imām Muḥammad al-Mahdī ﷺ. This question presupposes that she is ignorant of her identity; however, the reason behind Ḥakīmah's question is the absence of the signs of pregnancy [on Narjis], as she states, so her question came as a means of astonishment and confirmation of the news. All this is evident in the following that was narrated by Ḥakīmah:

> "So I stayed at his house [Imām Ḥasan al-'Askarī ﷺ] until sunset, then I called for my bondmaid to hand me my clothes so that I can leave.
>
> However, he ﷺ said:
>
>> Do not leave, aunt, stay the night at our house, for tonight a newborn will be born, who is most precious to God ﷻ and through whom God ﷻ will revive the earth after its death.

[90] Ṣadr, Sayyid Muḥammad Muḥammad Ṣādiq, *Mawsu'at al-Imām al-Mahdī* ﷺ, Vol. 1, p. 260.

So I asked:

> Who is his mother, my master, for I do not see any signs of pregnancy on Narjis?

He said:

> It is Narjis and no other.

So I hurried to her and turned her over onto her back, but I could not see any sign of pregnancy. No one knew of it until the time came for her to give birth because the Pharaoh used to cut open pregnant women in his persecution of Prophet Mūsā ﷺ, and this [newborn] is equal to Mūsā [in their situations]."[91]

Hence, the only argument against this narration remains in its chain of narrators and the unknown men, preventing it from being reliable. However, this can be refuted by observing the following reports:

The author of *Dalā'il al-Imāmat* reported the following:

"Abū al-Ḥusayn Muḥammad b. Hārūn told me: My father ﷺ narrated to me: Abū 'Alī Muḥammad b. Hammam narrated to us: Ja'far b. Muḥammad narrated to us: Muḥammad b. Ja'far told us about Abū Na'īm, on the authority of Muḥammad b. al-Qāsim al-'Alawī, he said:

---

[91] Ṣadūq, Shaykh Muḥammad b. 'Alī, *Kamāl al-Dīn wa Tamām al-Ni'ma*, p. 427.

We entered a group of ʿAlawīyūn upon Ḥakīmah, daughter of Muḥammad b. ʿAlī b. Mūsā ﷺ, and she said:

> You have come to ask me about the birth of the Vicegerent of God?

We said:

> Yes, by God.

She said:

> He was with me yesterday, and he told me about it and that I had a girl called (Narjis); I used to raise her among the bondmaids, and no one else could raise her but me."[92]

Furthermore, the author of *Ithbāt al-Waṣīyah* reported another account with different transmission chains that indicate the same meaning:

> "A group of scholarly Shaykhs, including Allān al-Kilābī, Mūsā b. Muḥammad al-Ghazī, and Aḥmad b. Jaʿfar b. Muḥammad with their chains of transmission, narrated that Ḥakīmah, the daughter of Abū Jaʿfar ﷺ and aunt of Abū Muḥammad ﷺ, used to pray that God grant Abū Muḥammad ﷺ, a son whenever she entered upon him and that she said:

[92] al-Ṭabarī, Muḥammad b. Jarīr, *Dalāʾil al-Imāmat*, p. 499.

One day, I entered upon him and prayed for him as I always do, so he said to me:

> O aunt, the newborn we were expecting will be born tonight, on the night of the middle of Shaʿbān in the year 255, so break your fast with us. It was a Friday night.

I asked him:

> Who is the mother of this newborn, my master?

He replied:

> Your bondmaid, Narjis."[93]

The narration clearly states that she was a bondmaid of Ḥakīmah ﷺ. More importantly, the author of *Ithbāt al-Waṣīyah* also highlighted that this report is narrated extensively, meaning there are other narrations. Therefore, this is in line with what al-Khaṣībī reported in his book *al-Hidāya al-Kubrā*, where he not only stated how this account is cited extensively but also reported it in detail with the entirety of its chains of transmission as follows:

Hārūn b. Muslim b. Saʿdan al-Basrī, Muḥammad b. Aḥmad b. Muṭahar al-Baghdādī, Aḥmad b. Isḥāq, Sahl b. Ziyād al-Ādamī, ʿAbdullāh b. Jaʿfar al-Hamīrī, Aḥmad b. Abī

---

[93] al-Hudhalī, ʿAlī b. Ḥusayn al-Masʿūdī, *Ithbāt al-Waṣiyyah lil Imām ʿAlī b. Abī Ṭālib* ﷺ, p. 272.

ʿAbdullāh al-Barqī, Ṣāliḥ b. Muḥammad al-Hamadānī, Jaʿfar b. Ibrāhīm b. Nūḥ, Dawūd b. ʿĀmir al-Ashʿarī al-Qummī, Aḥmad b. Muḥammad al-Khaṣībī, Ibrāhīm b. al-Khaṣīb, Muḥammad b. ʿAlī al-Bashrī, Muḥammad b. ʿAbdullāh al-Yaqtīnī al-Baghdādī, Aḥmad b. Muḥammad al-Nīshābūrī, Aḥmad b. ʿAbdullāh b. Mahrān al-Anbarī, Aḥmad b. Muḥammad al-Sayrafī, ʿAlī b. Bilāl, Muḥammad b. Abī al-Sahbānī, Isḥāq b. Ismāʿīl al-Nīshābūrī, ʿAlī b. ʿUbaydullāh al-Ḥasanī, Muḥammad b. Ismāʿīl al-Ḥusaynī, Abū al-Ḥusayn Muḥammad b. Yaḥyā al-Fārsī, Aḥmad b. Sindol, al-ʿAbbās al-Labbān, ʿAlī b. Ṣāliḥ, ʿAbdul Ḥamīd b. Muḥammad, Muḥammad b. Yaḥyā al-Kharqī, Muḥammad b. ʿAlī b. ʿUbaydullāh al-Ḥasanī, Ibn ʿAsīm al-Kūfī, Aḥmad b. Muḥammad al-Ḥajal, ʿAskar (the servant of Abū Jaʿfar the ninth Imām), al-Zayyān (the servant of al-Riḍā), Ḥamza (the servant of Abū Jaʿfar the ninth Imām), ʿĪsā b. Mahdī al-Jawharī, al-Ḥasan b. Ibrāhīm, Aḥmad b. Ismāʿīl, Muḥammad b. Maymūn al-Khurāsānī, Muḥammad b. Khalaf, Aḥmad b. Ḥasān, ʿAlī b. Aḥmad al-Ṣāʾigh, al-Ḥasan b. Masʿūd al-Furātī, Aḥmad b. Ḥayyān al-Ajlī, al-Ḥasan b. Mālik, Aḥmad b. Muḥammad b. Abī Qurna, Jaʿfar b. Aḥmad al-Qāṣir al-Basrī, ʿAlī b. al-Ṣabūnī, Abū al-Ḥasan ʿAlī b. Bishr, al-Ḥasan al-Balkhī, Aḥmad b. Ṣāliḥ, al-Ḥusayn b. ʿAṭāb, ʿAbdullāh b. ʿAbdul Bārī, Aḥmad b. Dawūd al-Qummī, Muḥammad b. ʿAbdullāh, Ṭālib b. Ḥātim b. Ṭālib, al-Ḥasan b. Muḥammad b. Masʿūd b. Saʿd, Aḥmad b. Marān, Abū Bakr al-Saffār, Muḥammad b. Mūsā al-Qummī, ʿAṭāb b. Muḥammad al-Daylamī, Aḥmad b. Mālik al-Qummī, Abū Bakr al-Jawārī, and ʿAbdullāh, all of which were in close proximity of the two Imāms عليهما السلام,

narrated on the authority of our masters Abū al-Ḥasan [Imām 'Alī al-Hādī] and Abū Muḥammad [Imām Ḥasan al-'Askarī] ﷺ [...]

Abū Muḥammad ﷺ said:

> I invited my aunts into my home, so I saw a bondmaid of theirs; she had been adorned, and she was called Narjis.

I looked at her for a long time, so my aunt Ḥakīmah said:

> My master, I see that you are gazing intently at this bondmaid.

So I said:

> O aunt, I only look at her out of amazement for God has willed her to bear from His goodness and Will.

She said:

> My master, I feel that you want her.

I said yes and told her to get permission from my father 'Alī b. Muḥammad ﷺ so that I can have her.

She did so, and he ﷺ ordered her the same, so she brought Narjis to me.

al-Ḥusayn b. Ḥamdān said:

> "It was narrated to me by those who added the names of those who narrated to me from these men whom I name, and they are Ghaylān al-Kilābī, Mūsā b. Muḥammad al-Rāzī, and Aḥmad b. Jaʿfar al-Ṭūsī, on the authority of Ḥakīmah, the daughter of Muḥammad b. ʿAlī al-Riḍā 🌸...".[94]

## She Was Born in the ʿAlawī Household

Referring to the oldest sources available at hand, we encounter another crystal-clear truth: Imām Muḥammad al-Mahdī's mother 🌸 was born in the ʿAlawī household, specifically in the home of Ḥakīmah 🌸, and she was not bought into it from the slave market. Proof of this is what the author of *Ithbāt al-Waṣīyah* mentioned:

> "Our trusted scholars narrated to us that one of the sisters of Abū al-Ḥasan ʿAlī b. Muḥammad 🌸 had a bondmaid born in her home and whom she raised; she was called Narjis."[95]

---

[94] Khaṣībī, Ḥusayn b. Ḥamadān, *al-Hidāyat al-Kubrā*, p. 353.

[95] al-Hudhalī, ʿAlī b. Ḥusayn al-Masʿūdī, *Ithbāt al-Waṣiyyah lil Imām ʿAlī b. Abī Ṭālib* 🌸, p. 272.

The value of this report lies in the following matters:

First: al-Masʿūdī died in the year 346 AH, after less than 100 years from the birth of Imām Muḥammad al-Mahdī ﷺ. He witnessed the time of the minor occultation, and he even lived in Baghdād where the deputies, may God sanctify their pure souls, were present. As such, his reports would be much more reliable and accurate than Shaykh Muḥammad b. ʿAlī Ṣadūq, Shaykh Muḥammad b. Ḥasan Ṭūsī, and others as they emerged in later times, and some of them in places further away as well.[96]

Second, He reported this account through one means and highlighted the extensiveness of the transmission by using the term "scholars", meaning that there were at least three people. The scholars of al-Masʿūdī's league undoubtedly witnessed this account as well.

Third: Most importantly, he testified about the reliability of his transmission means and did not keep silent about them. Hence, even if they were unknown to us, we know

[96] This book is famously attributed to al-Masʿūdi, author of *Murūj al-Dhahab wa Maʿādin al-Jawhar*; however, some investigators in this matter doubted the authenticity of this attribution, suggesting that it is instead authored by al-Shalmaghānī and titled *al-Awṣiyāʾ*. Based on the known attribution of the book to al-Masʿūdī, you can recognize the [high] academic value of the narration. On the other hand, if you were to adhere to the attribution of the book to al-Shalmaghānī, then the narration acquires an even higher academic value as he had authored books in the period of the minor occultation and he was close to the deputies.

their status [reliability] based on al-Masʿūdi's testimony about them.

Furthermore, the author of the book *ʿUyūn al-Muʿjizāt* reported the same narration with an insightful difference; he said:

> "I read in many books from different authentic perspectives that Ḥakīmah, the daughter of Abū Jaʿfar Muḥammad b. ʿAlī ﷺ had a bondmaid who was born in her house and whom she raised, and she was called Narjis. When she grew up, Abū Muḥammad once entered upon her and gazed at her, so his aunt Ḥakīmah said:
>
>> My master, I see that you are looking at her.
>
> He ﷺ said:
>
>> I only look at her out of amazement as she will bear a son most precious to God.
>
> He then told Ḥakīmah to get permission from his father Abū al-Ḥasan [Imām ʿAlī al-Hādī] ﷺ to nudge her [Narjis] to him, so she did, and Abū al-Ḥasan told her to do so."[97]

This transmission of the report adds to what has been presented two points:

---

[97] Ibn ʿAbd al-Wahhāb, Shaykh Ḥusayn, *ʿUyūn al-Muʿjizāt*, p. 127.

First: The scholar of ḥadīth Ḥusayn b. ʻAbdul Wahhab ﵀, who had lived at the time of al-Sharīf al-Murtaḍā ﵀, attested to the authenticity of the narrations that reported the birth of Narjis ﵍ in the house of Ḥakīmah. Regardless of whether we infer that he meant the narrator's trustworthiness or the narration's content, it remains sufficient as historical evidence.

Second, He highlighted the extensiveness of the account's transmission in the books of the companions, where he said, "I read in many books..." This indicates that this account was famous and widespread in the companions' books that fell in his hands.

Combining these two points, we conclude that it was a famous, well-known, and well-transmitted report among the companions during the minor occultation that Imām Muḥammad al-Mahdī's mother ﵍ was born in the home of Lady Ḥakīmah ﵍.

## Other Supporting Clues

Among other matters that reinforce what we have theorized is that it matches the state of the Imām's mother ﵍, providing us with an appropriate conception of her:

- She was born in Islam.
- She was raised in the Holy House [among the Ahl al-Bayt ﵍].

- She was disciplined by Ḥakīmah 🌿, the daughter of Imām Muḥammad al-Jawād 🌿.

- No man had touched her, and she was not revealed to anyone before.

This contrasts the narration of al-Raḥnī, which, if we were to accept, would set forth several issues that do not suit the status of Imāmate:

- She was born on polytheism.

- She was raised in the court of tyranny.

- A slave dealer owned her.

- She was new to Islam.

Do these characteristics suit the mother of the Seal of Vicegerents 🌿, who will fill the earth with peace and justice just as oppression and corruption have been rampant?

## The Full Picture Thus Emerges

All that was presented proves that Imām Muḥammad al-Mahdī's mother 🌿 is a Nubian bondmaid born in the house of Ḥakīmah 🌿, the daughter of Imām Muḥammad al-Jawād 🌿, who took it upon herself to raise and discipline her until she gave her to Imām Ḥasan al-'Askarī 🌿—based on his request—during the lifetime of his father Imām 'Alī al-Hādī ؑ. Nobody knew of her pregnancy until the last night when the light of God emerged on His earth.

Furthermore, all this also invalidates al-Raḥnī's narration, which we discussed in previous chapters, and contradicts all these clear and authentic narrations. We can thus deem it to be the composition of storytellers at that time.

# Her Status Among the Ahl al-Bayt ؑ

Undoubtedly, the mothers of the infallible ؑ are of special status and position to God, the Exalted, for He chose them to bear His signs to mankind [Ḥujaj] and custodians in His lands. Such trust can only be given to those who are loyal and devoted such that God elevates and picks them over the rest of His creation.

In this chapter, we will mention how the Ahl al-Bayt ؑ spoke about the mother of al-Qā'im ؏:

## What Was Narrated on the Authority of God's Messenger ﷺ?

In this regard, Shaykh Muḥammad b. Ya'qūb Kulaynī ؒ narrated with his chain of transmission:

"The Messenger of God ﷺ said:

> May my father be sacrificed for the son of the best of the bondmaids, the son of the sweet-mouthed Nubian who was chosen to give birth to this purified son.
>
> May the curse of God be upon the 'Ubaydīs [the 'Abbāsids] and their descendants, the instigators of strife [fitnah], and may they suffer greatly and be subject to torture, humiliation, and death for years, months, and days [at the hand of al-Qā'im when he reappears or by God]. He is the one in occultation,

> the one who was persecuted and left without a home, the one who could not avenge the blood of his father and his grandfather.
>
> People wonder: did he die or perish? What path did he walk?
>
> O uncle, he is undoubtedly from me [my descendant].

So I said:

> You are truthful; may I be sacrificed for you."[98]

## What Was Narrated on Amīr al-Mu'minīn's ﷺ Authority?

In his book *al-Ghaybah*, al-Nu'mānī narrated with his chain of transmission on the authority of al-Ḥārith al-Awar al-Ḥamdāni that Amīr al-Mu'minīn ﷺ said:

> "May my father be sacrificed for the son of the best of bondmaids—meaning al-Qā'im ﷺ from his descendants—he shall subject them to humiliation and pain and death upon his sword; at that point, the wicked of Quraysh shall wish that they could be spared

[98] Kulaynī, Shaykh Muḥammad b. Ya'qūb, *al-Kāfī*, Vol. 1, p. 322.

from the world and what is in it so that they would be forgiven. We will not stop them until God is pleased."⁹⁹

In another narration reported by al-Jawharī with a chain of transmission on the authority of Abī Juhayfa al-Sawā'ī—from Sawā'a b. 'Āmir—al-Ḥarith b. 'Abdullāh al-Jarthī al-Hamdānī, and al-Ḥarith b. Sharb, all of them narrated that whenever they were with Imām 'Alī b. Abī Ṭālib 🕮 and his son Imām al-Ḥasan 🕮 came upon them; he would say:

Greetings, O son of the Messenger of God 🕮.

Whenever his son [Imām] al-Ḥusayn came upon them, he would say:

May my father and mother be sacrificed for you, O father to the son of the best of bondmaids.

So it was said to him:

O Amīr al-Mu'minīn, why do you say that to [Imām] al-Ḥasan and this to [Imām] al-Ḥusayn? And who is the son of the best of bondmaids?

He answered:

The one who is missing and persecuted, left without a home, Muḥammad [Imām Muḥammad al-Mahdī 🕮] b. al-Ḥasan b. 'Alī b. Muḥammad b.

---

⁹⁹ Ṭūsī, Shaykh Muḥammad b. Ḥasan, al-Ghaybah, p. 234.

> ʿAlī b. Mūsā b. Jaʿfar b. Muḥammad b. ʿAlī b. Imām al-Ḥusayn ﷺ.

As he said this, he placed his hand upon [Imām] al-Ḥusayn's ﷺ head.

## What Was Narrated on Imām al-Ḥasan's ﷺ Authority?

Shaykh Muḥammad b. ʿAlī Ṣadūq ﷺ narrated with his chain of transmission:

> "When Imām al-Ḥasan b. ʿAlī ﷺ made peace with Muʿāwīya b. Abī Sufyān, the people entered upon him. Some of them condemned him for his pledge of allegiance, so he ﷺ said:
>
> > You do not know what I did, by God, I have only done what is good for my Shīʿa everywhere [...], did you not know that none of us is free from the burden of pledging to the tyrants of our time, except for al-Qāʾim ﷺ, behind whom the Spirit of God ʿĪsā b. Maryam ﷺ, for God ﷻ, will hide his birth and conceal him so that he does not bear the burden of allegiance to anyone if he emerges. The ninth of the offspring of my brother [Imām] al-Ḥusayn, the son of the lady of bondmaids, God will prolong his life in his occultation, and then He will reveal him with His Power in the form of a young

man below 40 years of age; indeed, God is capable of everything."[100]

## What Was Narrated on Imām Muḥammad al-Bāqir's ﷺ Authority?

In his book *al-Ghaybah*, Shaykh Muḥammad b. Ḥasan Ṭūsī ﷺ narrated the following:

"On the authority of Jābir al-Ja'fī, he said:

> I heard Abū Ja'far ﷺ say: 'Umar b. al-Khattab asked Amīr al-Mu'minīn ﷺ:
>
> > Tell me about al-Mahdī, what is his name?
>
> So he said:
>
> > As for his name, my beloved swore me not to speak of his name until God sends him forward.
>
> 'Umar said:
>
> > What about his characteristics?

---

100 Ṣadūq, Shaykh Muḥammad b. 'Alī, *Kamāl al-Dīn wa Tamām al-Ni'ma*, p. 316.

He replied:

> He is a young man of medium stature, a beautiful face, and beautiful hair that flows over his shoulders, and the light [Nūr] in his face shines over the black hair of his beard and hears; may my father be sacrificed for the son of the best of bondmaids."[101]

Another report is narrated on his ؑ authority, reinforcing that this conversation is indeed referring to Imām Muḥammad al-Mahdī's mother ؑ, where al-Nuʿmānī narrated with his chain of transmission to ʿAbd al-Raḥīm al-Qāṣir:

"I said to Abū Jaʿfar ؑ:

> When Amīr al-Muʾminīn ؑ said "the son of the best of bondmaids", did he mean Fāṭimah ؑ?

So he said:

> Rather, Fāṭimah ؑ is the best of the free women. He [al-Mahdī] has a broad abdomen and a red face. May God have mercy upon so-and-so."[102]

---

[101] Ṭūsī, Shaykh Muḥammad b. Ḥasan, *al-Ghaybah*, p. 470.

[102] Ibid, p. 233.

## What Was Narrated on Imām Jaʿfar al-Ṣādiq's ﻋﻠﻴﻪ ﺍﻟﺴﻼﻡ Authority?

Shaykh Muḥammad b. ʿAlī Ṣadūq ﻗﺪﺱ ﺳﺮﻩ narrated with his chain of transmission on the authority of Abī Basir:

"I heard Abū ʿAbdillah ﻋﻠﻴﻪ ﺍﻟﺴﻼﻡ say:

al-Qāʾim from us the Ahl al-Bayt follows in the path of the prophets ﻋﻠﻴﻬﻢ ﺍﻟﺴﻼﻡ in terms of what befell them of occultations the same.

So I said:

O son of the Messenger of God, who is al-Qāʾim from among you, Ahl al-Bayt?

He said:

O Abū Basīr, he is the fifth offspring of my son Mūsā, the one who is the son of the lady of bondmaids, and he shall vanish into an occultation that will scare the deceivers. Then God ﻋﺰ ﻭﺟﻞ will reveal him; through him, He shall conquer the east and the west of the earth and the Spirit of God ʿĪsā b. Maryam ﻋﻠﻴﻪ ﺍﻟﺴﻼﻡ will descend to earth and pray behind him. Earth will shine with the light of its Lord, and every corner of this world will be filled with the worship of God and no other, and religion will

> belong entirely to God, even if the polytheists abhorred this."[103]

## What Was Narrated on Imām Mūsā al-Kāẓim's ﷺ Authority?

Shaykh Muḥammad b. ʿAlī Ṣadūq with his chain of transmission on the authority of Abī Aḥmad Muḥammad b. Ziyād al-Azadī:

> "I asked my master Mūsā b. Jaʿfar about the saying of God:
>
> ﴿وَأَسبَغَ عَلَيكُم نِعَمَهُ ظاهِرَةً وَباطِنَةً﴾
>
> ﴿*wa-ʾasbagha ʿalaykum niʿamahū ẓāhiratan wa-bāṭinatan*﴾
>
> ﴿*and He has showered upon you His blessings, the outward and the inward*﴾[104]
>
> So he said:
>
> The outward blessing is the seen Imām, and the inward blessing is the concealed Imām.

---

[103] Ṣadūq, Shaykh Muḥammad b. ʿAlī, *Kamāl al-Dīn wa Tamām al-Niʿma*, p. 346.

[104] Sūrat Luqmān, Verse 20.

I said to him:

Will one of the Imāms be concealed?

He said:

Yes, he will be concealed from the eyes of the people, but his remembrance will not vanish from the hearts of the believers. He is the twelfth Imām from among us, and God will ease every difficulty and hardship for him, and He will show him all the treasures of the earth and bring near to him everything far away. Through him, God will expunge every relentless tyrant, and every rebellious devil will perish at his hand. He is the son of the lady of bondmaids, the one whose birth was hidden from the people and whose name people are not permitted to utter until God 🕮 reveals him so that he fills the earth with peace and justice just as it had been rampant with corruption and oppression."[105]

Furthermore, the scholar of ḥadīth al-Nūrī reported on the authority of Yūnus b. ʿAbd al-Raḥmān, he said:

"I entered upon Mūsā b. Jaʿfar 🕮 and said:

O son of the Messenger of God, are you the one who establishes justice?

---

[105] Ibid., p. 368.

He said:

> Indeed, I am. However, al-Qā'im, who will purify the earth from the enemies of God and fill it with justice just as it had been rampant with oppression, is the fifth of my offspring. And so on until he said: He is the twelfth [Imām] from among us, and God will ease every difficulty and hardship for him, and He will show him all the treasures of the earth and bring near to him everything far away. Through him, God will expunge every relentless tyrant, and every rebellious devil will perish at his hand. He is the son of the lady of bondmaids, the one whose birth was hidden from the people and whose name people are not permitted to utter until God ﷻ reveals him so that he fills the earth with peace and justice just as it had been rampant with corruption and oppression."[106]

## What Was Narrated on Imām 'Alī al-Riḍā's ؑ Authority?

Shaykh Muḥammad b. 'Alī Ṣadūq ؒ narrated with his chain of transmission on the authority of al-Ḥusayn b. Khālid:

---

[106] Ṭabrisī, Mīrzā Ḥusayn Nūrī, *Mustadrak al-Wasā'il wa-Mustanbaṭ al-Masā'il*, Vol. 12, p. 282.

"ʿAlī b. Mūsā al-Riḍā ﷺ said:

> He who has no piety has no religion, and he who has no Taqiyyah [precautionary dissimulation or denial of religious belief and practice] has no faith, the best of you in front God are those who practice Taqiyyah.

So it was said to him:

> O son of the Messenger of God, until when?

He said:

> Until the known day, and it is the day when our Qāʾim from Ahl al-Bayt emerges, so he who abandons Taqiyyah before the emergence of our Qāʾim is not from [among] us.

It was said to him:

> O son of the Messenger of God, who is al-Qāʾim from among you, Ahl al-Bayt?

He said:

> The fourth from my offspring, the son of the lady of bondmaids, through him, God will purify the

> earth from every injustice and sanctify it against every oppression."[107]

## What Was Narrated on the Authority of Ḥakīmah, Daughter of Imām Muḥammad al-Jawād ﷺ?

Finally, we shall conclude with what was narrated on the authority of the pure Lady Ḥakīmah ﷺ, who transmitted to us what happened in the house of Imām Ḥasan al-ʿAskarī ﷺ, as she put forth several matters that demonstrate to us the status of the mother of Imām Muḥammad al-Mahdī among the holy progeny:

Shaykh Muḥammad b. ʿAlī Ṣadūq ؒ reported the following narration on her ﷺ authority:

> "She [Ḥakīmah] said:
>
> > Abū Muḥammad al-Ḥasan b. ʿAlī [Imām Ḥasan al-ʿAskarī] ﷺ called for me and said:
> >
> > > O aunt, break your fast with us tonight; it is the night of the middle of Shaʿbān. God ﷻ will reveal His Ḥujjah [sign to mankind] to His earth this night.

---

[107] Ṣadūq, Shaykh Muḥammad b. ʿAlī, *Kamāl al-Dīn wa Tamām al-Niʿma*, p. 371.

So I said to him:

> Who is his mother?

He answered me:

> Narjis.

I said to him:

> May I be sacrificed for you, but she does not show any signs [of pregnancy].

He said:

> It is indeed as I am telling you.

So I came, and when I greeted her and sat down, she came to take off my slippers and said to me:

> O my mistress and the mistress of my family, how are you?

So I said to her:

> Rather, you are my mistress and the mistress of my family.

She rejected this and said:

> What is this that you are saying, O aunt?

I said:

> O, daughter, God The Almighty will bestow upon you in your night a son who is a master in this world and the Hereafter. At that, she became humble and shy."[108]

In another wording, Ḥakīmah said:

> "Abū al-Ḥasan [Imām ʿAlī al-Hādī] عليه السلام left, and Abū Muḥammad عليه السلام sat in his father's place, and I used to visit him as I used to visit his father.
>
> One day, Narjis came to remove my slippers, and she said:
>
> > O my mistress, give me your slippers.
>
> So I said:
>
> > Rather, you are my mistress; by God, I will not allow you to take my slippers off or to serve me, for I shall gladly serve you instead."[109]

---

[108] Ibid., p. 424.

[109] Ibid., p. 427.

## The Crux of the Matter

The presented narrations lead us to important conclusions that can be summarized as follows:

First: No women from the Ahl al-Bayt ﷺ has been mentioned in such a significant number of narrations except for the Lady of the Women Sayyidah Fāṭimah al-Zahrā' ﷺ, to whom no other woman is comparable. Despite the magnificence of the fate of the rest of the women of the Ahl al-Bayt ﷺ, we do not find such many narrations in their right. This extensiveness in the number of narrations indicates Ahl al-Bayt's great concern for this pure lady ﷺ.

Second: The narrations above focused on one trait: the fact that she is the best of the bondmaids or the lady of the bondmaids. The repetition of this trait by more than one Imām over their different periods points to her being at the top of goodness, for she is the absolute best of all bondmaids. Just as Sayyidah Fāṭimah al-Zahrā' ﷺ is the foremost lady of all women of the words, Narjis ﷺ is the lady of the bondmaids of the worlds, including all bondmaids, even Ḥajar, the mother of Ismā'īl ﷺ.

Third: The characteristics that the Holy Prophet ﷺ mentioned in her right lead us to dedicate a prolonged look into this personality. He ﷺ described her as "sweet-mouthed", distinguishing her from all other women as the meaning here is not fresh smelling or dainty and lovely, for that is a trait shared by many women; instead, the actual meaning here is what al-Māzandarānī ﵀ stated: her speech [mouth] being free of evil vain talk and falsehood [laghw] and polytheism [shirk].[110] Second, he ﵇ described her as the one "which was chosen to give birth to the purified one," once again highlighting how God chose her for this great purpose and mission.

As such, it becomes clear why Ḥakīmah ﵍ called Narjis ﵍ her mistress and the mistress of her family, for the excellent lady ﵍ understood from the talk that she heard from the infallible ﵇ the greatness of this woman and her elevated status to God, as she was favored over the most extraordinary ladies of the infallible Ahl al-Bayt ﵈. Hence, this ʿAlawī daughter, sister, and aunt of the Imāms bows to kiss the hand of this pure mother whose status God elevated in this world and the Hereafter. Perhaps even more narrations have not reached us and demonstrate her ﵍ great stature.

---

[110] al-Māzandarānī, al-Mawlā Muḥammad Ṣāliḥ, *Sharḥ Uṣūl al-Kāfī*, Vol. 6, p. 212.

# Her Death

In this chapter, we shall investigate a most critical and sensitive matter: her 🌸 fate after giving birth to the Imām of the Time 🌸. This topic is often overlooked due to the mixup between essential events related to the lives of both noble Imāms 🌸. So, what happened afterward?

## Her Death in the Life of Imām Ḥasan al-ʿAskarī 🌸

Some claimed that the pure lady 🌸 died during the lifetime of Imām Ḥasan al-ʿAskarī based on a narration mentioned by Shaykh Muḥammad b. ʿAlī Ṣadūq 🌸 in *Kamāl al-Dīn*, where he said:

"Muḥammad b. ʿAlī Mājīlūwī 🌸 narrated to us: Muḥammad b. Yaḥyā al-ʿAṭṭār narrated to us:

> Abū ʿAlī al-Khayzarānī told us about a bondmaid of his whom he had given to Abū Muḥammad 🌸; when Jaʿfar al-Kadhāb [i.e., the liar] raided the house, she escaped back to him [from Jaʿfar], and he thus married her.

Abū ʿAlī then said:

> She told me that she had attended the birth of the Master 🌸, that his mother is called Ṣāqīl, and that Abū Muḥammad 🌸 had told her [Ṣāqīl] about what was happening to his children, so she asked to him to invoke God 🌸 to make it so that she meets her death before him. And so, she died in the lifetime of Abū Muḥammad 🌸, and on her grave,

> there is a slab upon which (this is the grave of Umm Muḥammad) is written."[111]

However, it is tough to build upon this narration and rely on it in such a case, and that is due to the following:

First: The first issue is the presence of unknown men (Abī ʿAlī al-Khayzarānī) in the chain of narrators, as there is no mention of this man in the biography books, indexes, and history books; hence, he is unknown to us in essence and state, and he has no narration in the books of the companions except for this narration, which is the matter of conflict.

Second: The second issue is the unknown identity of this bondmaid that al-Khayzarānī talked about. She claimed that she attended the birth [of Imām Muḥammad al-Mahdī ﷻ] and heard what went on between Imām Ḥasan al-ʿAskarī ﷺ and Imām Muḥammad al-Mahdī's mother ﷺ and that she was present during the raid of Jaʿfar al-Kadhāb and had succeeded in escaping... All these matters warrant her popularity among the elite and the authorities that used to enforce special monitoring of all women of the Imām's ﷺ household, as will be discussed later.

Third: If we were to overlook all these issues, there remains a more profound dilemma at hand: the possibility that the purpose behind promoting this story was to hide the tracks

---

[111] Ṣadūq, Shaykh Muḥammad b. ʿAlī, *Kamāl al-Dīn wa Tamām al-Niʿma*, p. 431.

of Imām Muḥammad al-Mahdī's mother ﷺ and protect her from the malice of the hostile enemies. As you will see, there are numerous reports that she was alive after the martyrdom of Imām Ḥasan al-ʿAskarī ﷺ, and she had a confrontation with the authorities. Such an account [the one under discussion above] is not fit to contradict the consensus among the sect about her life; thus, it is most viable to consider that what al-Khayzarānī reported is just for the sake of covering up the tracks of the pure Lady Narjis ﷺ.

## Her Staying Alive After the Martyrdom of Imām Ḥasan al-ʿAskarī ﷺ

This is a matter of almost complete consensus among the sect, as well as historians, as they mentioned the events that occurred after the passing of Imām Ḥasan al-ʿAskarī ﷺ and what calamities she ﷺ endured, treating these events as universal truths. In this regard, citing what al-Najashī ﵀ wrote on Muḥammad b. ʿAlī b. Ḥamza al-ʿAbbāsi is sufficient.

> "Muḥammad b. ʿAlī b. Ḥamza b. al-Ḥasan b. ʿUbaydullāh b. al-ʿAbbās b. ʿAlī b. Abī Ṭālib ﷺ Abū ʿAbdullāh, a trustworthy person of righteous belief and a chief in the field of ḥadīth, has a narration on the authority of Abū al-Ḥasan [Imām ʿAlī al-Hādī] and Abū Muḥammad [Imām Ḥasan al-ʿAskarī] ﷺ and a written correspondence, and the mother of Ṣāḥib al-Amr ﷺ [one of the titles of Imām Muḥammad al-

> Mahdī; means 'lord of the cause'] stayed in his home after the death of al-Ḥasan [Imām Ḥasan al-'Askarī] عليه السلام."[112]

He clearly stated that she عليها السلام lived after Imām Ḥasan al-'Askarī عليه السلام and that many events occurred necessitating her to seek refuge and protection in the house of the trustworthy 'Alawī.

More important is what Shaykh Muḥammad b. 'Alī Ṣadūq رحمه الله reported in *Kamāl al-Dīn* about her witnessing the death of Imām Ḥasan al-'Askarī عليه السلام and staying alive after him, where he said:

> "I found proof in some books compiled in the histories, and I heard it solely on the authority of Muḥammad b. al-Ḥusayn b. 'Ibād that he said:
>
> > Abū Muḥammad al-Ḥasan b. 'Alī [Imām Ḥasan al-'Askarī] عليه السلام died on a Friday with the morning prayer, and on that night, he had written by hand many letters to Madīnah, and that was on the eighth of the month of Rabī' al-Awwal in the year 260 AH. At that time, with him were only Ṣāqīl, the bondmaid, and 'Aqīd, the servant, and only God عزوجل knows who else. 'Aqīd requested water boiled with mastic, and we brought it to him.

---

[112] al-Najāshī, Aḥmad, *al-Fihrist*, p. 248.

Then he ﷺ said:

> I will start praying, so prepare me.

So we laid a towel on his lap, and he took the water from Ṣāqīl to wash his face and arms and wiped his head and feet before praying the morning prayer in his bed. He took the cup to drink, but the cup hit his teeth as his hand trembled and shook, so Ṣāqīl took it from his hand, and he passed away after—God's blessings be upon him. He was buried at his house in Ṣurrah Man Ra'ā [i.e., today known as Sammara] next to his father, ﷺ. So he went to God The Exalted at the age of 29 years."[113]

The importance of his words is two-fold:

On the one side, its importance lends itself to his mention of the popularity of this text in the historical hooks that came before him, i.e., in the period of the minor occultation as is known, in addition to hearing of this event from Muḥammad b. al-Ḥusayn b. ʿIbād.

On the other side, Shaykh Muḥammad b. ʿAlī Ṣadūq also reported al-Khayzarānī's report about her ﷺ death in the lifetime of Imām Ḥasan al-ʿAskarī ﷺ, and this prevents us from assuming that he relies on this former report,

[113] Ṣadūq, Shaykh Muḥammad b. ʿAlī, *Kamāl al-Dīn wa Tamām al-Niʿma*, p. 474.

hence invalidating the claim that it is possible that she ﷺ died and was buried early.

In addition to all those above, it is also prudent to consider the numerous events that historians have proven, and that shed light on what happened to her ﷺ after the passing of Imām Ḥasan al-ʿAskarī ﷺ, which thus invalidates the theory of her early death.

## The Crux of the Matter

The well-established and known fact that cannot be refuted is that Lady Narjis ﷺ stayed alive after the death of Imām Ḥasan al-ʿAskarī ﷺ. The presence of one narration that contradicts this historically known matter does not discredit it, even if it were considerable—but that is not the case as demonstrated above (the narration suffers several issues as it).

# Her Jihād

After validating the fact that the mother of our master Imām Muḥammad al-Mahdī ﷺ remained after Imām Ḥasan al-ʿAskarī ﷺ, we arrive now at the most essential side of the life of this pure lady ﷺ: her Jihād during the minor occultation and protection of the Imām of our Time ﷺ. To demonstrate the truth, it is prudent to present the events from the beginning:

## The Martyrdom of Imām Ḥasan al-ʿAskarī ﷺ

The first vital discussion to lead with is the martyrdom of Imām Ḥasan al-ʿAskarī ﷺ due to the ʿAbbāsid poison—the narration reported by Shaykh Muḥammad b. ʿAlī Ṣadūq ﷺ indicates that she ﷺ was with him in his last moments:

> "Abū Muḥammad al-Ḥasan b. ʿAlī [Imām Ḥasan al-ʿAskarī] ﷺ died on a Friday with the morning prayer, and on that night, he had written by hand many letters to Madīnah, and that was on the eighth of the month of Rabīʿ al-Awwal in the year 260 AH. At that time, with him were only Ṣāqīl, the bondmaid, and ʿAqīd, the servant, and only God ﷻ knows who else. ʿAqīd requested water boiled with mastic, and we brought it to him.
>
> Then he ﷺ said:
>
>> I will start praying, so prepare me.
>
> So we laid a towel on his lap, and he took the water from Ṣāqīl to wash his face and arms and wiped his

> head and feet before praying the morning prayer in his bed. He took the cup to drink, but the cup hit his teeth as his hand trembled and shook, so Ṣāqīl took it from his hand, and he passed away after—God's blessings be upon him. He was buried at his house in Ṣurrah Man Ra'ā [i.e., today known as Sammara] next to his father. So he went to God at the age of 29 years."

What is important to note from this narration is that no one else besides her was at the side of our master Imām Ḥasan al-'Askarī except for "'Aqīd the servant" and Imām Muḥammad al-Mahdī. This reinforces her great closeness to Imām Ḥasan al-'Askarī over the other ladies of his household, and it also conveys that the Imām was preparing for another mission no less important than the previous ones. Proof of this is that the Imām knew of his demise beforehand and thus kept most of his household away, even his mother, such that only Lady Narjis remained.

The author of *Ithbāt al-Waṣīyah* narrated on behalf of Aḥmad b. Maslaqa said:

> "I entered upon Abū Muḥammad, so he said to me:
>
>> O Aḥmad, in what state were you when the people were engrossed in doubt and distrust?

So I said:

> When the letter came with the news of the birth of our Master 🕊, no man, woman, or child from among us reached this understanding except that they declared with the truth.

He 🕊 said:

> Did you not know that the earth will never be void of a Ḥujjah [sign] of God? Then Abū Muḥammad 🕊 ordered his mother to perform Ḥajj in the year 259 and told her of his fate in the year 260 [his death]. Then, he passed the great name, inheritances, and weapons to al-Qā'im 🕊. The mother of Abū Muḥammad 🕊 left for Ḥajj, and Abū Muḥammad 🕊 was martyred in the month of Rabīʿ ath-Thānī in the year 260. He was buried in Ṣurrah Man Ra'ā [i.e., Sāmarrā'] next to his father Abū al-Ḥasan [Imām ʿAlī al-Hādī] 🕊 at the age of 29."[114]

## The Plot of the ʿAbbāsid Insurgence

To understand what was going on during that period, it is necessary to know what Jaʿfar al-Kadhāb [i.e., the liar] did to the household of the Imām and the infallibles, as it appears that he was in a close relationship with the

---

[114] al-Hudhalī, ʿAlī b. Ḥusayn al-Masʿūdī, *Ithbāt al-Waṣiyyah lil Imām ʿAlī b. Abī Ṭālib* 🕊, p. 217.

'Abbāsid court at that time. In cooperation with them, he had been planning to take over the reins of Imāmate and assume leadership over the Shīʿa population at that time.

The groundwork of this insurgence had started taking root in the lifetime of Imām Ḥasan al-ʿAskarī 🕮, as some history books indicate the establishment of a whole faction of loyalists to Jaʿfar al-Kadhāb. Al-Qāḍī al-Nuʿmān documented the existence of this faction in his saying:

> "A faction of people pledged allegiance to Jaʿfar b. ʿAlī, and they rejected the Imāmate of al-Ḥasan [Imām Ḥasan al-ʿAskarī] in his life, saying: We tested him and found him not to know. When he died without leaving a son behind [as Imām Muḥammad al-Mahdī's birth was hidden], they complained, saying that an Imām is not an Imām unless he has an offspring and successor."[115]

The death of Imām Ḥasan al-ʿAskarī's 🕮 death presented the perfect opportunity for Jaʿfar al-Kadhāb to claim Imāmate as the Imām did not have an apparent son [as Imām Muḥammad al-Mahdī was hidden] who would succeed him and claim the Imāmate. Therefore, the faction that declared with the so-called Imāmate of Jaʿfar al-Kadhāb would gain influence as the [apparent] absence of a successor would be considered an indicator of the invalidity of the Imāmate of Imām Ḥasan al-ʿAskarī 🕮!

---

[115] al-Nuʿmān, al-Qāḍī, *Sharḥ al-Akhbār fī Faḍāʾil al-Aʾimma al-Aṭhār* 🕮, Vol. 3, p. 312.

As such, Ja'far al-Kadhāb seized the opportunity to make his grab for the Imāmate official by praying the funeral prayer for his brother Imām Ḥasan al-'Askarī ﷺ. However, the unexpected happened as Imām Muḥammad al-Mahdī ﷺ appeared suddenly and dismantled his plans when he came forward and prayed for his father, revealing himself to the people.

In this regard, Shaykh Muḥammad b. 'Alī Ṣadūq reported on the authority of Abī al-Adyān a long account, in which the following was mentioned:

> "I set out to the Madā'in with the letters and collected the responses to them, and I entered Ṣurrah Man Ra'ā on the fifteenth as he ﷺ had told me; at his house, I found that the Imām had passed and that Ja'far b. 'Alī, his brother, was standing at the door of his house with Shī'a around him, offering condolences and congratulations as well.
>
> So I thought to myself:
>
>> If he [Ja'far] is the Imām, then the Imāmate has indeed ended, for I have seen that he drinks wine, gambles, and plays the tanbūra [musical instrument]. I came forward and offered my condolences and congratulations, yet he did not ask me about anything.

Then, ʿAqīd emerged and said:

> O my master, your brother has been shrouded; come and lead the funeral prayer for him.

So Jaʿfar b. ʿAlī entered and with him the Shīʿa, at the fore of which were al-Sammān and al-Ḥasan b. ʿAlī Qātil al-Muʿtasim, who is known as Salma. Inside the house, we saw al-Ḥasan b. ʿAlī [Imām Ḥasan al-ʿAskarī] ﷺ shrouded. Jaʿfar b. ʿAlī stepped forward to lead the funeral prayer for his brother. When he started with takbīr, a boy with a wheatish complexion, short curly hair, and cleaved teeth emerged and grabbed the mantle of Jaʿfar b. ʿAlī, and he said:

> Step aside, uncle, for I have more right to lead the prayer for my father.

So Jaʿfar stepped aside, his face losing color and clouding. The boy then stepped forward and offered the funeral prayer for him, and then the Imām was buried next to his father's grave ﷺ.

Then he [the boy] said:

> O Basrī, give me the letters' responses with you.

So I gave them to him and thought to myself:

> These are two prophecies fulfilled thus far, and now what remains is the one about the bag's content.

I then went to Jaʿfar b. ʿAlī who was exhaling heavily, so Ḥājiz al-Washa told him:

My master, who is this boy so that I can establish an argument against him?

He said:

By God, I have never seen or known him. While we were sitting, a group from Qum came and asked about al-Ḥasan b. ʿAlī [Imām Ḥasan al-ʿAskarī] 🌸. When they learned of his death, they asked whom to offer condolences.

The people indicated Jaʿfar b. ʿAlī greeted him, consoled him, and congratulated him, and then they said:

We have letters and money; tell us, from whom are these letters, and how much money do we carry?

He [Jaʿfar] got up, dusting off his clothes and exclaiming:

You want me to know the unseen?

Then the servant came out of the house and said:

You have the letters of so-and-so, and the belted purse of money contains one thousand dinars, only ten pure.

So they gave him the letters and the money and said:

> Whoever sent you [with this information] must be the [real] Imām."[116]

## Opposing the Liar

The ʿAbbāsid plan was ultimately foiled by the appearance of Imām Ḥasan al-ʿAskarī's 🕮 boy, who was hidden from the public. So, Jaʿfar al-Kadhāb [i.e., the liar] could only report the matter to his ʿAbbāsid benefactor al-Muʿtamid, and he incited him to get rid of the boy. Thus came the first assault on the house of Imām Ḥasan al-ʿAskarī 🕮.

Shaykh Muḥammad b. ʿAlī Ṣadūq 🕮 reported:

> "Jaʿfar b. ʿAlī entered upon al-Muʿtamid and told him of the matter. Al-Muʿtamid then gave orders to his servants to capture the bondmaid Ṣāqīl. They interrogated her about the boy, but she denied it, and she claimed to be pregnant to cover up the state of the boy. So she was given to Ibn Abī al-Shawārib al-Qāḍī. However, the death of ʿUbaydullāh b. Yaḥyā b. Khāqān came unexpectedly, and Ṣāḥib al-Zanj [the leader of the Zanj revolt against the ʿAbbāsids] emerged in al-Baṣrah; thus, they got busy handling these matters and were

---

[116] Ṣadūq, Shaykh Muḥammad b. ʿAlī, *Kamāl al-Dīn wa Tamām al-Niʿma*, p. 476.

distracted from the bondmaid, so she was able to flee them, praise be to God."[117]

In another text, the following was narrated:

"When she received the news, the mother of Abū Muḥammad ﷺ—her name is 'ḥadīth'—came from Madīnah to Ṣurrah Man Ra'ā, and there were many long stories about her encounters with the Imām's brother Ja'far, including how he demanded his inheritance and how he sought to bring her to the Sulṭān and reveal the matter that God ﷻ had ordered to be hidden. At that, Ṣāqīl claimed that she was pregnant, so she was taken to the property of al-Mu'tamid, where his women and servants, al-Muwaffaq's women and servants, and al-Qāḍī b. Abī Shawārib's women and servants monitor her at all times. However, they were suddenly bombarded with the matter of al-Saffār, the unexpected death of 'Ubaydullāh b. Yaḥyā b. Khaqān, their exit from Ṣurrah Man Ra'ā, and the matter of Sāḥib al-Zanj in al-Baṣrah; thus, they got busy and distracted from her."[118]

Here, the first real mission that this pure lady ﷺ undertook emerges: when the 'Abbāsids raided her house and arrested her, she claimed that she was pregnant for two reasons. First, it was to cover up for the boy whom the 'Abbāsids

[117] Ibid.

[118] Ibid.

wanted to get rid of, as it was difficult to merely take the word of Ja'far al-Kadhāb about Imām Ḥasan al-'Askarī 🕮 having a son in the presence of the tight monitoring that was enforced on that house. Second, without the existence of a son of Imām Ḥasan al-'Askarī 🕮, the people would accept the claim of Ja'far without examining it or giving it any thought. However, the presence of another potential contender makes the matter different as people will seek to investigate and uncover the truth, which is not in the interest of Ja'far al-Kadhāb, for he is a man of debauchery and corruption. He would be quickly revealed as such.

According to this text, her imprisonment by the 'Abbāsids extended until after the death of 'Ubaydullāh b. Yaḥyā b. Khaqān died in the year 263 AH, as historians have mentioned. Hence, she spent three years in the 'Abbāsid prison!

Instead, it was even reported that her imprisonment went on for more than this duration, as Ibn Ḥazm reported that she spent seven years in prison, where he said:

"She claimed to be pregnant after her master al-Ḥasan b. 'Alī [Imām Ḥasan al-'Askarī 🕮], his inheritance was halted for seven years, and his brother Ja'far b. 'Alī disputed her on it. A group of government elites took her side, and another took the side of Ja'far. Then, the pregnancy was exposed to be false, and Ja'far took his brother's inheritance. The death of al-Ḥasan [Imām Ḥasan al-ʿAskarī ﵇] happened in the year 260."[119]

## The Period of Hiding

It appears that the release of Lady Narjis ﵇ did not happen by the will of the ʿAbbāsid court; instead, it seems to be an escape from the prison as suggested by the phrases reported by Shaykh Muḥammad b. ʿAlī Ṣadūq, including

> "they got busy handling these matters and were distracted from the bondmaid, so she was able to flee them" and "they got busy and distracted from her".

In particular, Ibn Ḥazm also indicated the presence of cooperators with Lady Narjis ﵇ inside the ʿAbbāsid court as he said:

> "A group of the government leaders took her side."[120]

Furthermore, the reports of Shaykh Muḥammad b. ʿAlī Ṣadūq ﵀ highlights the circumstances that contributed to her escape as he conveyed a group of grave political events that affected the power of the ʿAbbāsid government and its control over matters, and these events are as follows:

---

[119] Ibn Ḥazm, *Kitāb al-Faṣl fī al-Milal wal-Ahwā' wal-Niḥal*, Vol. 4, p. 77.

[120] Ibid.

- The intensification of the Zanj revolution

- The emergence of Layth b. Yaʿqūb al-Saffār

- The death of ʿUbaydullāh b. Yaḥyā b. Khaqān

From this point onward, this pure lady ☝ entered into a period of hiding, fearing arrest, and that is why she did not return to the house of Imām Ḥasan al-ʿAskarī ☝. Instead, she roamed the earth, fleeing the gaze of the ʿAbbāsids, and her state in this period was indicated in the following narration reported by Shaykh Muḥammad b. Yaʿqūb Kulaynī ☝ with his chain of transmission on the authority of Aḥmad b. Isḥāq, where he said:

"It is forbidden for you to ask about that name, and I do not say this from my account, for I cannot set what is permissible and what is forbidden. But this was an order from him [Imām Ḥasan al-ʿAskarī] ☝, as the Sulṭān thinks that Abū Muḥammad did not leave an offspring behind after his death and that his inheritance was divided and taken by those who have no right to it. His family is dispersed about, and no one dares to introduce themselves to them or give them anything. If the name is uttered, the search for them commences, so fear God and do not speak of it."

Hence, it appears that Jaʿfar al-Kadhāb monopolized the entirety of his brother's inheritance, Imām Ḥasan al-ʿAskarī ☝, and the Imām's blessed family was left with no place to settle in. Therefore, after the escape of the pure Lady Narjis 🕊 from her prison, she did not return to her house and instead started to move between the houses of the significant Shī'a in 'Irāq.

The first abode in which the pure lady 🕊 settled was the house of Muḥammad b. 'Alī b. Ḥamza al-'Abbāsi, whom al-Najashī wrote about in his book *al-Fihrist* and mentioned her 🕊 stay at his house as follows:

"Muḥammad b. 'Alī b. Ḥamza b. al-Ḥasan b. 'Ubaydullāh b. al-'Abbās b. 'Alī b. Abī Ṭālib 🕊 Abū 'Abdullāh, a trustworthy person of righteous belief and a chief in the field of ḥadīth, has a narration on the authority of Abū al-Ḥasan [Imām 'Alī al-Hādī] and Abū Muḥammad [Imām Ḥasan al-'Askarī] 🕊 and a written correspondence, and the mother of Ṣāḥib al-Amr 🕊 [one of the titles of Imām Muḥammad al-Mahdī; means 'lord of the cause'] stayed in his home after the death of al-Ḥasan [Imām Ḥasan al-'Askarī] 🕊."[121]

Historians reported that he died in the year 287 AH, including al-Marzabānī, who said:

"He was a poet, a storyteller, and a scholar who narrated many accounts from his family and cousins,

---

[121] al-Najāshī, Aḥmad, *al-Fihrist*, p. 248.

> and he had met with many of our Shaykhs who told us about him. He died in the year 287."[122]

It seems that she left this house after the death of its owner ﵀, perhaps due to the absence of someone who could ensure her safety and security, especially since the ʿAbbāsid authorities persecuted her. Proof of this is that Ibn Ḥazm reported that she ﵇ was arrested more than 20 years after the death of her master, essentially before 290 AH or instead 289 AH as she was arrested in the time of al-Muʿtaḍid who died in this year. She was arrested in the house of al-Ḥasan b. Jaʿfar al-Nawbakhtī, the famous ʿAbbāsid scribe.[123]

Combining all these matters, we can conclude that Lady Narjis ﵇ left the house of Muḥammad b. ʿAlī b. Ḥamza ﵀ and moved into al-Nawbakhtī's house, staying there for a year or some more before she was arrested there and imprisoned once again.

## To the ʿAbbāsid Prison!

As demonstrated, Lady Narjis ﵇ was imprisoned for the second time. In this regard, Ibn Ḥazm also reported some of the events of this imprisonment in his book *Kitāb al-Faṣl fī al-Milal wal-Ahwāʾ wal-Niḥal* as follows:

---

[122] al-Marzabānī, Muḥammad b. ʿImrān, *Muʿjam al-Shuʿarāʾ*, p. 453 .

[123] Ibn Ḥazm, *Kitāb al-Faṣl fī al-Milal wal-Ahwāʾ wal-Niḥal*, Vol. 4, p. 77.

"The Rāwāfiḍ's sedition against Ṣāqīl and her advocacy grew increasingly until al-Muʿtadid imprisoned her after more than 20 years since the death of her master. And it was censured that she was staying in the house of al-Ḥasan b. Jaʿfar al-Nawbakhtī, the scribe, so she was found there and forcibly taken to the palace of al-Muʿtadid, where she stayed until her death in the period of al-Muqtadir."[124]

This text presents several points to consider:

First, The pure lady ☙ ended up settling in the house of al-Ḥasan b. Jaʿfar al-Nawbakhtī was a scribe for the ʿAbbāsids, and we do not rule out the possibility that this was the work of the third deputy al-Ḥusayn b. Rūḥ al-Nawbakhtī ☙ was working under the command of the second deputy, Muḥammad b. ʿUthmān al-Amri ☙. He belonged to Banī Nawbakht and was very pious and trusted by everyone.

Second: It appears that the ʿAbbāsids discovered the hiding place of Lady Narjis ☙ by way of denunciation inside the ʿAbbāsid court, and this is inferred from the saying:

"And it was censured that she was staying in the house of al-Ḥasan b. Jaʿfar al-Nawbakhtī, the scribe, so she was found there..."

---

[124] Ibid.

The expression "so she was found there" indicates they had been oblivious to her presence before that. History does not report the fate of al-Nawbakhtī after that.

Third, Important to note is the type of imprisonment that she was subject to at this time. In this regard, Ibn Ḥazm reported that she was held captive in the palace of the Caliph, not in the prison of the common people (proof: "...and [she was] forcibly taken to the palace of al-Muʿtadid where she stayed..."). This highlights the criticality of the Mahdīst cause in the eyes of the ʿAbbāsids at that time and their diligence in foiling the Mahdīst movement.

Fourth: Through this text, one can also pinpoint the duration of her imprisonment. Previous reports indicated that the beginning of her imprisonment was between the years 287 and 288 AH. She stayed in this prison until she met her death during the days of al-Muqtadir, who took over the reins of the Caliphate in the year 295 AH. Hence, she was imprisoned for at least seven years before her death.

## Why Such Imprisonment?

In this section, we shall discuss the crux of Ibn Ḥazm's report, his saying:

> "The Rāwāfiḍ's sedition against Ṣāqīl and her advocacy grew increasingly..."

This highlights that she was active among the Shīʿa circles at that time, more than 20 years after the martyrdom of Imām Ḥasan al-ʿAskarī ﷺ. This raises a baffling question: what was her ﷺ role during that period?

In this regard, there are three possibilities:

The first possibility is that Lady Narjis ﷺ escaped from the ʿAbbāsid prison in the events above and stayed on the authorities' wanted list. The ʿAbbāsids's search for her intensified in the period of the Caliph al-Muʿtamid because of his fanaticism against the Ahl al-Bayt ﷺ and their Shīʿa, and perhaps their focus on this pure lady was because they aimed to use her to pressure Imām Muḥammad al-Mahdī ﷺ and make his arrest easier.

The second possibility is that Lady Narjis ﷺ was absent from the public this entire extended period and then resurfaced at the forefront of events as a result of the influx of disgraceful occurrences, such as the emergence of many who claimed falsely to be deputies in the time of [the real deputy] Muḥammad b. ʿUthmān al-Amrī ﷺ, as her reappearance and support for him strengthens his position against the imposters and unifies the word of the Shīʿa of the Ahl al-Bayt ﷺ.

The third possibility is that she did not disappear from the forefront of events at all in the first place; instead, she was secretly active behind the scenes, as it is possible that she was the link connecting the Imām عليه السلام with other people, even including al-Amri and his son!

While we do not have proof of the first and second possibilities, evidence favors the third. Reviewing the texts available at hand, we find indicators of a secret network of women demonstrating critical activism that is equal to the work of the four deputies:

Among these women is Ḥakīmah, the aunt of Imām Ḥasan al-ʿAskarī عليه السلام. She used to work on proving that her nephew عليه السلام had offspring and that all doubters and skeptics would come to her for proof. Many narrations and reports were mentioned previously in her right, so repetition is unnecessary.

Another woman from among them is the mother of Abū Muḥammad, the grandmother of Imām Muḥammad al-Mahdī. The narrations indicate her role in the minor occultation, as Shaykh Muḥammad b. ʿAlī Ṣadūq رحمه الله reported the following with his chain of transmission on the authority of Aḥmad b. Ibrāhīm:

> "I entered upon Ḥakīmah, the daughter of Muḥammad b. ʿAlī al-Riḍā and sister of Abū Ḥasan al-ʿAskarī عليهما السلام, in the year 282 in Madīnah.
>
> I talked to her from behind a veil and asked her about her religion, so she named [the Imāms] whom she follows and said:

> So-and-so, the son of al-Ḥasan [Imām Ḥasan al-ʿAskarī] ﷺ.

Then she mentioned his name, so I asked her:

> May God sacrifice me for you. Did you witness this yourself or receive this news as a report?

She said:

> A report from Abū Muḥammad ﷺ, which he wrote to his mother.

So I said to her:

> Where is the newborn?

She said:

> Hidden.

I said:

> To whom do the Shīʿa resort to [for guidance]?

She said:

> To the grandmother, the mother of Abū Muḥammad ﷺ.

I asked her,

> Whom has he emulated in appointing a woman as his deputy?

So she said:

> He follows the example of [Imām] al-Ḥusayn b. ʿAlī b. Abī Ṭālib, for [Imām] al-Ḥusayn b. ʿAlī put his sister Sayyidah Zaynab, the daughter of [Imām] ʿAlī b. Abī Ṭālib, in charge in his stead in the apparent, and so any knowledge from [Imām] ʿAlī b. al-Ḥusayn [Imām Zayn al-ʿĀbidīn] is attributed to Sayyidah Zaynab, daughter of ʿAlī, to maintain a veil of secrecy and cover [for protection] on [Imām] ʿAlī b. al-Ḥusayn."[125]

Another among these women is the old lady who appears to have been the aunt of the awaited Imām. In his book *al-Ghaybah*, Shaykh Muḥammad b. Ḥasan Ṭūsī narrated an account with his chain of transmission on the authority of Yaʿqūb b. Yūsuf al-Dharrāb al-Ghasānī, on his departure from Isfahan, said:

> "I performed Ḥajj with a group of people of opposing beliefs [i.e., Sunnīs] from my town in 281 AH. When we reached Makkah, one of our companions rented us a house on Sūq al-Layl Street, and the house was a

[125] Ṣadūq, Shaykh Muḥammad b. ʿAlī, *Kamāl al-Dīn wa Tamām al-Niʿma*, p. 501.

property of Lady Khadījah عليها السلام, which was known as Dār al-Riḍā عليه السلام. The house was occupied by an old lady who had a dark complexion. When I learned that the house was called Dār al-Riḍā عليه السلام, I asked that old lady how she was related to the house owner and why it was called Dār al-Riḍā.

She said,

> I am one of the adherents of the house's owner, and this house belongs to ʿAlī b. Mūsā al-Riḍā عليه السلام. Imām Ḥasan al-ʿAskarī عليه السلام has accommodated me because I had been in his service.

I was delighted upon hearing that, but I did not disclose the information to the [Sunnī] people with me. Whenever I returned from Ṭawāf at night, I slept in the corridor with them. We used to close the door and place a massive stone behind it. One night, I saw a light in the corridor where we slept; it was similar to the light of a lantern. Then the door was opened, but I did not see anyone from the people of the house opening it. I saw a young man with medium stature and a wheatish complexion; he seemed physically fit and had a prostration mark on his forehead. He wore two shirts, a cloak he cast over his head, and shoes without socks. The man entered and climbed up to the room [or attic] that the old lady occupied. She had told us not to go up there as her daughter was in it.

When the man went up to the room, I noticed that the light in the corridor was now up there, although I did not exactly see any lantern [...] Curiosity overcame me; I wanted to know about this man. I asked the old lady about him and told her,

> O so-and-so, I want to ask you something in private, but I cannot do it as others are also present. So, when you notice that I am alone in the house, I would like it if you could come down so that I can ask you about something.

She replied hurriedly,

> I also want to speak to you in private, but I have not had the chance because of those accompanying you.

I asked,

> What did you want to tell me?

She said,

> He—[but she did not mention anyone]— has told you not to be harsh with your companions and associates and do not dispute with them, for they are your enemies, and it is their house.

I asked,

> Who has said this?

She replied,

> I do.

I dared not ask anything else since a sort of awe and fear had entered my heart. I just asked what she meant by companions. I thought she was implying my present companions with whom I had come for Ḥajj.

But she said,

> Your associates in your town and those with you in the house.

In truth, I had had disputes with my companions in the house with me about religious matters. They began gossiping about me until I ran away from there and went into hiding. Now I understood that she was talking about them.

I asked,

> What is your relation to [Imām] al-Riḍā ﷻ?

She said,

> I was the servant of [Imām] al-Ḥasan b. ʿAlī ﷻ.

When I became certain that she was connected to that family, I asked her about the Imām in Occultation [al-Ghayb] ؑ and said,

> I beseech you, tell me if you have seen him yourself!

She said,

> O brother, I have not seen him with my own eyes because when I had left that place, my sister was pregnant, al-Ḥasan b. ʿAlī [Imām Ḥasan al-ʿAskarī] ؑ had given me the glad tidings that I would see him at the end of my life, and he told me:
>
> > You will be to him as you were to me.
>
> After that, I would see him descend from the room many nights with the light accompanying him. I used to open the door and follow the light, but I could only see the light, and that person would remain invisible to me until he reached the masjid. Moreover, I used to see men from various cities visit this house and hand over letters to that old lady, and I saw her handing them letters [of response] as well, and they would speak to each other, but I could not understand them. I also encountered some of

> them on the way back home till I reached Baghdād.[126]

Overall, all these texts collectively indicate that al-Amrī and his son (the first two deputies) were known for their close relationship with the holy progeny, especially since Ja'far al-Kadhāb had exposed all the secrets of the network of agents that was under the control of Imām Ḥasan al-'Askarī ﷺ. As an alternative, it was prudent to establish another network for the agents to act as a nexus connecting them with the rest of the [Shī'a] populace. The women ultimately fulfilled this role, at the forefront of which was the pure Lady Narjis ﷺ. On this note, I suspect that the person who ratted her whereabouts out was one of the agents who had turned against Muḥammad b. 'Uthmān al-Amri and who everyone trusted. Unfortunately, we do not have enough information and evidence on this matter.

Nonetheless, we might possess evidence of this supposition: the selection of the third deputy al-Ḥusayn b. Rūḥ al-Nawbakhtī. Shaykh Muḥammad b. Ḥasan Ṭūsī ﵀ reported that he [the third deputy] did not know of any significant matters and particularities among the agents of Imām Muḥammad al-Mahdī.

In this regard, Shaykh Muḥammad b. Ḥasan Ṭūsī ﵀ narrated with his chain of narrators on the authority of Ja'far b. Aḥmad b. Maṭil:

---

[126] Ṭūsī, Shaykh Muḥammad b. Ḥasan, *al-Ghaybah*, p. 273.

> Muḥammad b. ʿUthmān Abū Jaʿfar al-Amri ﷺ had about ten individuals under his command who carried out his work, among which was Abū al-Qāsim b. Rūḥ ﷺ. However, all of them were closer to him than Abū al-Qāsim b. Rūḥ, to the extent that if he needed something done, he would send the others to fulfill it as Abū al-Qāsim b. Rūḥ did not have a proximity to him. When Abū Jaʿfar ﷺ passed away, Abū al-Qāsim b. Rūḥ was chosen to be appointed [as deputy]."[127]

Furthermore, Shaykh Muḥammad b. Ḥasan Ṭūsī also said:

> "Our Shaykhs said: We thought undoubtedly that if Abū Jaʿfar were to pass away, only Jaʿfar b. Aḥmad b. Maṭil or his father would take his place, for he was very close to him and would always frequent his house, to the extent that towards the end of his life, Abū Jaʿfar would only eat food prepared at the house of Jaʿfar b. Aḥmad b. Matīl and his father, due to an incident that had occurred. Hence, his meals were at the house of Jaʿfar and his father, and our companions never doubted that if he were to pass away, Jaʿfar b. Aḥmad b. Maṭil would be appointed in his place. However, when Abū Jaʿfar passed, and Abū al-Qāsim was chosen instead, they did not reject it; rather, they stood with him and at his service just as they were with Abū Jaʿfar ﷺ. And Jaʿfar b. Aḥmad b. Matīl continued to serve Abū al-Qāsim just as he had served Abū Jaʿfar al-Amri

[127] Ibid., p. 369.

> until his death ﷺ. Thus, anyone who would criticize Abū al-Qāsim would be criticizing Abū Jaʿfar and thus the Ḥujjah [one of the titles of Imām Muḥammad al-Mahdī, i.e., God's proof or sign to humanity], God's blessings be upon him."[128]

In light of our analysis, the reason for which al-Ḥusayn b. Rūḥ was chosen was the fact that the news of him being Shīʿa was not widespread among the people of ʿIrāq due to his expertise in performing Taqiyyah [precautionary dissimulation or denial of religious belief and practice]. In this regard, Shaykh Muḥammad b. Ḥasan Ṭūsī ﷺ reported that Abū ʿAbdullāh b. Ghālīb, the father-in-law of Abū al-Ḥasan b. Abū al-Ṭayyib, said:

> "I have not seen anyone wiser than Shaykh Abū al-Qāsim al-Ḥusayn b. Rūḥ. I saw him one day in Ibn Yasar's house. He had great standing with the Caliph al-Muqtadir, and the populace [i.e. (Ahl al- Sunnah) revered him. Abū al-Qāsim used to attend that place due to Taqiyyah and fear. I remember once when two people were arguing; one was saying that Abū Bakr was the best of people after the Messenger of God ﷺ, followed by ʿUmar and then ʿAlī, while the other was saying that ʿAlī was better than ʿUmar.
>
> Their argument thus exacerbated, so Abū al-Qāsim ﷺ said:

[128] Ibid.

> The Ṣaḥābah agreed unanimously that al-Ṣiddīq [Abū Bakr] comes first, then al-Fārūq ['Umar], followed by 'Uthmān of the two lights and then 'Alī the Successor. Narrators of ḥadīth maintain the same, which is the correct belief according to us.

The attendees were perplexed by his words, and most of the populace (from Ahl al- Sunnah) praised and prayed for him, criticizing anyone who would accuse him of being a Rāfiḍī."[129]

Furthermore, it has been reported about him ﷺ what is even more significant than those above:

"Shaykh Abū al-Qāsim ﷺ came to know that his doorman had cursed Mu'āwīya, so he ordered his expulsion from his service. The doorman kept asking him to reinstate him for a long time, but by God, Abū al-Qāsim did not. Someone else gave him employment instead; all this was done to maintain Taqiyyah."[130]

Ultimately, the covertness of this network of women, which was headed by the pure Lady Narjis ﷺ, necessitated the appointment of the deputy who had other characteristics, the most important of which is that all sides accept him and has a standing with them and that he is not

---

[129] Ibid, p. 384.

[130] Ibid., p. 386.

a matter of doubt or skepticism by the different groups of the population.

## Conclusion

The pure Lady Narjis عليها السلام played a significant role in the period of the minor occultation; however, history did not document for us the details of this great Jihād that she undertook in that era, and what we have mentioned is nothing but an attempt at compiling historical bits and pieces scattered across different books.

# Results of the Research

Following this brief tour of history and biographies, we can summarize the most important results we have obtained in the following bullet points:

First: The discrepancies between the narrations on the name of the mother of Imām Muḥammad al-Mahdī are not considered an issue in specifying the identity of this woman; instead, this is a matter that can be explained in several ways that were discussed in detail.

Second: There is no truth to the famous story about Lady Narjis coming from the lands of the Romans, and we have mentioned several issues that permeate the chain of narrators [sanad] and content [matn] of this account, thus leaving it void of any academic value.

Third: The narrations reported on the authority of the holy progeny prove that Lady Narjis was a Nubian bondmaid born in the house of Lady Ḥakīmah who took it upon herself to raise and discipline her so that she became the consort of Imām Ḥasan al-ʿAskarī and the mother of the Imām of the Time.

Fourth: Lady Narjis lived long after Imām Ḥasan al-ʿAskarī, and she was subject to many forms of ʿAbbāsid persecution, falling in imprisonment more than once and meeting her death during her imprisonment in the palace of the ʿAbbāsid caliphs.

Fifth: Historical texts contain some indicators that convey her significant role during this period [minor occultation];

however, the information must reveal the complete truth due to the lack of reported texts.

Ultimately, this is the summation of what we have reached via this tour, and we pray to God that we have done this great figure some part of the justice due in her right and that He blesses us with her Ziyārat in this world and her intercession in the Hereafter, for He is the Praiseworthy, the Glorious.

www.ingramcontent.com/pod-product-compliance
Lightning Source LLC
Chambersburg PA
CBHW031516120626
46545CB00005B/1897
*9781956276497*